EFT for
MEDITATION

by Charles B. Crenshaw Jr., MS and
Carol E. Crenshaw, MS, EdM

Energy Psychology Press
3340 Fulton Rd, #442, Fulton, CA 95439
www.EFTUniverse.com

Cataloging-in-Publication Data

Names: Crenshaw Jr., Charles B. | Crenshaw, Carol E.
Title: EFT for meditation / by Charles B. Crenshaw Jr. and Carol E.
    Crenshaw
Description: First editon. | Santa Rosa, CA: Energy Psychology Press,
    2017.
Identifiers: ISBN 978-1-60415-262-3 | ISBN 978-1-60415-263-0 (ebook)
Subjects: LCSH: Meditation | EFT (Emotional Freedom Techniques) —
Psychology. | Self-actualization — Psychology. | Spiritual life.

The autonomic nervous system illustration on page 94 and the lung illustration on page 112 reprinted with permission by Jennifer Hollis, MS, www.hollisvisualizations.com

Cover design by Victoria Valentine
Editing by Stephanie Marohn • Typesetting by Karin Kinsey
Typeset in Cochin and Adobe Garamond
First Edition • Printed in USA by Bang Printing
10 9 8 7 6 5 4 3 2 1

reader or user has done so with informed consent. The information is provided on an "as is" basis without any warranties of any kind, express or implied, whether warranties as to use, merchantability, fitness for a particular purpose, or otherwise.

The authors, publisher, and contributors to this book, and their successors, assigns, licensees, employees, officers, directors, attorneys, agents, and other parties related to them (a) expressly disclaim any liability for and shall not be liable for any loss or damage including but not limited to use of the information; (b) shall not be liable for any direct or indirect compensatory, special, incidental, or consequential damages or costs of any kind or character; (c) shall not be responsible for any acts or omissions by any party including but not limited to any party mentioned or included in the information or otherwise; (d) do not endorse or support any material or information from any party mentioned or included in the information or otherwise; and (e) will not be liable for damages or costs resulting from any claim whatsoever. The within limitation of warranties may be limited by the laws of certain states and/or other jurisdictions and so some of the foregoing limitations may not apply to the reader who may have other rights that vary from state to state. If the reader or user does not agree with any of the terms of the foregoing, the reader or user should not use the information in this book or read it. A reader who continues reading this book will be deemed to have accepted the provisions of this disclaimer.

Please consult qualified health practitioners regarding your use of EFT.

Contents

Introduction

We had been meditators for most of our lives, trained directly by an acknowledged meditation master from the Himalayas, when some friends mentioned that we might be interested in Emotional Freedom Techniques (EFT), also called "tapping." What we didn't know is that we were already familiar with the origins of EFT through our work with our local chiropractor and friend, Dr. Mark Knight, who had been a student of Dr. George Goodheart. The foundations for EFT came from Dr. Goodheart's work. Roger Callahan, the founder of a precursor to EFT (Thought Field Therapy, or TFT), and other notables in the Energy Psychology field built upon that foundation.

Our friends' suggestion led us to experiment with tapping on minor upsets in our lives and how EFT could advance our meditation practice. We were already acquainted with the efficacy of energy medicine, having used homeopathy under the guidance of highly trained homeopathic physicians. Charles' experience with prescribed constitutional homeopathic remedies was that every time there was the resolution of some problem, something extraordinary happened. Some subtle aspect of his meditation practice improved, whether it was a deepening of the breath or an added stillness to body or mind.

For example, after Charles was given a remedy for an aging prostate, his meditation practice and his hatha yoga practice (note: all the various "styles" of yoga teach the same poses and this is hatha yoga) improved in the ways just mentioned.

We submit that the remedy given worked on the physical as well as energetic level similar to the way EFT works on both the physical and energetic levels. We submit this analogy because this awareness plays an integral part in the rest of the story about a relationship between EFT and meditation.

Why EFT and meditation? As we will present in the pages to follow, meditation is something that can get us beyond our minds, in the ultimate sense. On the one hand, meditation, like psychotherapy (more commonly considered "talk therapy"), can be seen as a tool that helps us overcome our neuroses (a word not in common usage these days, basically meaning the conditioned debilitating ways we respond to life events). Psychotherapy, for example, helps us acclimate to our surroundings but can leave us a long way from understanding our true nature. Psychotherapy is a wonderful tool for those wanting to get along better in and with the world. EFT has come to be considered an adjunct to psychotherapy, and it can also be considered an adjunct to meditation, as will be shown as we progress through the book.

Part of our training in graduate school involved counseling and we were told, "If you want to be a counselor, you have to be in counseling, you have to undergo counseling." This is not unlike the instruction EFT practitioners are given to practice the Personal Peace Procedure, an EFT technique to clear all the upsetting memories of one's past. Practitioners need to be clear of any emotional turmoil that might interfere with their work with clients.

Charles' personal counseling experience with a clinical social worker on staff led him to memories of a disturbing interaction with his mother. A fascinating feature of human perception is that each individual perceives an event differently. The following account by Charles involves a mother's perception and that of an 8-year-old boy.

During my childhood, Disney aired the program *Zorro*. Senõr Zorro was a swashbuckling hero who fought the bad guys with his wits and a sword. His trademark was a Z swished into the clothes of his defeated foes. This fascinating macho hero who dressed in black, wearing a mask and cape, captured my imagination.

In the bathroom one morning, I noticed one of my father's double-edged razor blades lying in a tray on the shelf. I had never seen one loose before, only inside the razor that my dad used. I was then also fascinated by how my dad cut the hair off his face with his razor. I picked the blade up carefully and saw that it could cut newspaper quite easily. The thoughts of Zorro were always with me, and so I wondered if you could also use this razor blade to cut a Z in fabric like Zorro did. There was no fabric in the bathroom. Fortunate for my experiment, there was my mother's lovely vinyl shower curtain conveniently hanging in the tub. I swish, swish, swished a Z into my mom's new shower curtain! I swish, swish, swished another and another until there was no more space that I could reach.

I then looked around for something else to put the mark of Zorro on. There hung the matching curtains on the window and I found my way to making a few small marks on each curtain. I then went on my way, playing around the house with my regular toys. Needless to say, my mother wasn't happy when she saw the condition of her new bathroom curtains and shower curtain, and I paid the price for destroying them.

All the while I was being punished, I was trying to explain to someone playing the adult parent role what I have just explained to you. There was no malice in what I had done; it was only a small boy in wonder. Not having the words to support my position left me at a disadvantage in this situation and was the source of enough conflict within me that it came up in a therapy session during my graduate work.

Working with the therapist led me to call my mother to discuss the particulars of this event and the effect it had had on me. A bad idea. My effort caused an otherwise sweet little lady distress about a minor error she might have made in her long career as a mom!

Twenty-five years after that discussion with my mom about the ill-fated Zorro incident, I learned about

EFT. One afternoon, not long after discovering the technique, even before knowing about the Personal Peace Procedure, I was tapping on troubling events that had come up in my meditation practice. There the troubling Zorro episode with my mother surfaced.

I began to tap on the memory of not being able to communicate with my mom so long ago. As I did, a flood of sadness and hurt came forward. The sadness revolved around how I could not at the tender age of 8 express to my momma that I was not trying to hurt or get back at her, which was her perception at the time. I wept desperately, with nose running and mouth drooling, like a lonely child orphaned by parents due to some tragedy. This went on for several minutes as I let myself experience what was happening. After this period of emotional release, tapping throughout, I went about my day as usual. Come my regular meditation time, I noticed that something had changed.

Like my experience from getting a good homeopathic remedy, the emotional release from the tapping had provided me with an energetic opening, an expansion that I had not expected. My meditation practice improved on a subtle level. There was a subtle deepening of my breath experience and an added stillness in my body and mind.

Now, as with our experience with hypnosis and neuro-linguistic programming (NLP) before it, we sought to find out all we could about EFT. We explored the available trainings near where we live and found some not far away in the Minneapolis area. It is there that we met Dawson Church and found that his interest and our interest in helping humankind were similar.

Since that initial meeting, we pursued further training in EFT. One of the requirements was to read *The Promise of Energy Psychology: Revolutionary Tools for Dramatic Personal Change*, by David Feinstein, Donna Eden, and Gary Craig. In the acknowledgments, we ran across a familiar name: Dr. Martin Jerry. Dr. Jerry, like us, was an initiate in the meditative tradition of the Himalayan sages as represented by Sri Swami Rama. From the time we had begun studying and practicing EFT, we had pondered its relationship to the science of yoga and meditation. As we had been instructed, yoga and meditation are sciences.

How did EFT fit with the extraordinary capacity of meditation to elevate human consciousness? We contacted Dr. Jerry and he surprised us by sending along a book he had coauthored with his wife, Dr. Marian Jerry, and Swami Veda Bharati. The book explored the relationships between the science of yoga and what Dr. Jerry called "psychotechnologies," which included EFT. EFT is based on *prana vidya*, knowledge of the energy (*prana* or *chi*) body, though EFT does not use that language. This added fuel to the flame of our understanding that EFT could be a beneficial tool for meditators because of its stated goal of clearing the energy field of troubling thoughts and events. For us, this is the promise of EFT for meditators, and the promise of meditation for EFT practitioners. To be clear, the promise is that EFT is a tool that can help one "speed" through emotionally difficult and disturbing thought patterns, patterns that might hinder the progress of meditation, or even stop one from meditating altogether.

Throughout the book, we use the terms "adept," "meditation masters," and "ancients." These are our general terms for people who have left indications for us from ancient times about meditation and whose current representatives have submitted their bodies to scientific scrutiny. The subjective observations of the ancients have come down to us in the writings of acknowledged mystics and from other sources. These adepts were masters of the little traversed territory that is the mind-body complex. A point of contention in accepting or rejecting the findings of the ancients has always been the subjective nature of their experiences. As humans, we learn about new things by comparing them with things we know. In this book, we approach meditation from that perspective, noting that the definitions we give of meditation are based on the findings of the adepts.

1

About Meditation

What Is Meditation?

Our consideration of meditation is based on a simple definition: "a family of techniques which have in common a conscious attempt to focus attention in a nonanalytical way, and an attempt not to dwell on discursive, ruminating thought" (Shapiro, 1980). The word "contemplation" is commonly considered synonymous to meditation.

To Shapiro's simple definition, we would add that meditation is also characterized by withdrawal of the senses. What does it mean to withdraw the senses? This is actually something we all do on a regular basis. Every day, we go through the process of deleting things from our awareness. There is no way we can digest all the information coming through our five senses, so we naturally delete some. This is all done on a less than conscious level.

Recall the last time you were at a lecture, a sermon, or any place where you became distracted. You likely found yourself returning to an external awareness having missed some portion of what the speaker said. During the time of your mental flight, were you aware of hearing anything? Were you aware of seeing anything? External awareness of your surroundings, at least related to sight and sound, did not exist for that time period. In essence, what you did, on a less than conscious level, was disconnect your sense of hearing and seeing from the external environment. We do this also in dreaming sleep, deep dreamless sleep, and other periods of deep interiority.

Sense withdrawal is a prerequisite for the highest levels of meditation, per the adepts. In daily life, our senses move outward into the world, experiencing the world and taking in information through these faculties. With sense withdrawal, we turn our senses inward to focus within.

In general, there are two broad aspects to meditation: the "mundane," which relates to the health and self-regulation benefits of meditation; and the "supramundane," which refers to the altered states of consciousness that can result from meditation. They are the two wings of meditation's full flight. The outcomes of meditation, whether mundane or supramundane, transcend the boundaries of religion, philosophy, gender, ethnicity, sexual orientation, or any other human division.

The Benefits of Meditation

There is a large body of research on the benefits of a regular meditation practice. Specific studies are discussed in Chapter 3, but here is a quick list of how meditation can benefit you:

- Heightened immunity

- Decrease in illness
- Improved sleep
- Improved cardiac functioning
- Calmness
- Improved mood and better mood regulation
- Decrease in anxiety
- Reduction in symptoms of stress
- Improved cognitive function including memory, concentration, and reasoning

Why Combine EFT and Meditation?

Meditation is a tool that helps us make our way through the depths of what Swami Veda Bharati (a current-day meditation master and author of several books on meditation) calls the mind-field. The mind-field is all aspects of the mind, conscious and less than conscious. Per the adepts, meditation is the tool to help us understand ourselves on all levels. Along the way, we must learn the skill of nonattachment, or dispassion. This truly is one of the secrets to success in meditation. EFT, as will be shown, is a tool to help us develop dispassion, that is, nonattachment to disturbing life experiences. Learning the skill of dispassion takes time in meditation. A perplexing emotional event might take a while to resolve when we are learning dispassion. EFT could very well be the solution to getting beyond many negative emotional events quickly while also developing the much-needed skill of dispassion. As the adepts suggest, the proof of this contention can only be examined in your own mind-body laboratory!

Life's disturbing events can knock us off balance and disrupt our daily living as well as our meditation practice. Combining EFT practice with meditation practice can resolve the dilemma. EFT helps us release what is bothering us so we can peacefully sit for meditation. Meditation provides us with a means to fathom the depths of ourselves, achieving emotional purification along the way through dispassion. EFT can help with the emotional purification.

EFT Exercise:
Try Tapping after a Period of Meditation

This exercise will give you an idea of how EFT and meditation can function in association. Here is the basic process for using them together.

Choose a quiet spot to sit in an erect and comfortable position. Consider sitting still for a few minutes—just sitting still, nothing else. Adjust your sitting posture so that you feel free from the need to have to move for those few minutes.

Sit completely still without any conscious movement. Be aware that you are breathing and maintain this awareness for two to three minutes, that is, turn your attention to your breath, feeling your inhalations and exhalations.

As you sit and breathe, notice what comes before your mind's eye, what comes up from your less than conscious mind. Is there any memory that is even slightly emotionally disruptive? For some, this exercise might be aggravating; for others, an emotion will come forward relating to their thoughts; and for still others, there will be no noticeable emotion. Meditation as a practice sustained over time will reveal things in the less than conscious mind that this brief exercise might not. (Such revelations often hinder people from continuing the practice of meditation.)

If an uncomfortable thought, an experience tinged with a negative emotion, came to light, rate on a scale of 1 to 10 how strong the uncomfortable feeling is, with 1 being slight discomfort and 10 being extreme distress. As an example, let's say an interaction you had with your dad when you were a child came to mind and you felt some anger about it.

Tap on the side of your hand (see illustration of the side of the hand point) while saying something like:

Even though I'm angry at my dad for telling me I was wrong, I deeply and completely accept myself.

Tap on this until the rating of your distress lessens. When it lessens, tap through the eight tapping points, top of the head and then on the face and torso (see illustration), while repeating, "Angry," "Angry." You can do several rounds of these points if you find you are still feeling angry.

Side of the Hand Point

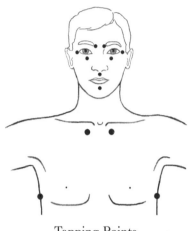

Tapping Points

Notice how you feel about the event now and then see if it disturbs you after two to three more minutes of sitting still.

For those who have no background in how to relax consciously, just tapping through the basic points a few times before doing this brief period of sitting still will produce a sense of relaxation that would make this exercise in mindfulness more pleasant. We will be discussing the ramifications of relaxation for meditation later in this book.

During the moments of sitting still, if your mind constantly wanders while you are focusing on your breath, you can tap on that. Tap on the side of the hand, saying something like:

Even though my mind constantly wanders when I watch my breath, I deeply and completely accept myself.

Even though it's hard for me to concentrate on my breath for more than a few seconds, I deeply and completely accept myself.

Even though thoughts of my daily life keep intruding on my breath, I deeply and completely accept myself.

Then tap on the other eight tapping points, saying phrases like these:

This difficulty following my breath.

It seems so easy.

But it isn't.

My mind constantly wanders off.

I forget about my breath.

Thoughts of daily life keep intruding.

It's so frustrating.

My mind wanders off after a few seconds.

There are many ways to approach and define meditation. Regardless of the path you follow, combining your approach with EFT will enhance both practices. The following chapter teaches the basics of EFT, for those who are new to the technique or would like a review.

2

How to Do EFT: The Basic Recipe by Dawson Church, PhD

Over the past decade, EFT has been the focus of a great deal of research. This has resulted in more than 20 clinical trials, in which EFT has been demonstrated to reduce a wide variety of symptoms. These include pain, skin rashes, fibromyalgia, depression, anxiety, and post-traumatic stress disorder (PTSD). Most of these studies have used the standardized form of EFT found in *The EFT Manual*. In this chapter, my goal is to show you how to unlock EFT's healing benefits in whatever physical or psychological problems you're facing. I have a passionate interest in relieving human suffering. When you study EFT, you quickly realize how much suffering can be alleviated with the help of this extraordinary healing tool. I'd like to place the full power of that tool in your hands, so that you can live the happiest, healthiest, and most abundant life possible.

If you go on YouTube or do a Google search, you will find thousands of websites and videos about EFT. The quality of the EFT information you'll find through these sources varies widely, however. Certified practitioners trained in EFT provide a small portion of the information. Most of it consists of personal testimonials by untrained enthusiasts. It's great that EFT works to some degree for virtually anyone. To get the most out of EFT and unlock its full potential, however, it's essential that you learn the form of EFT that's been proven in so many clinical trials: Clinical EFT.

Every year in EFT Universe workshops, we get many people who tell us variations of the same story: "I saw a video on YouTube, tapped along, and got amazing results the first few times. Then it seemed to stop working." The reason for this is that a superficial application of EFT can indeed work wonders. To unleash the full power of EFT, however, requires learning the standardized form we call Clinical EFT, which has been validated, over and over again, by high-quality research, and is taught systematically, step by step, by top experts, in EFT workshops.

Why is EFT able to produce beneficial results with so many problems, both psychological and physical? The reason for its effectiveness is that it reduces stress, and stress is a component of many problems. In EFT research on pain, for instance, we find that pain decreases by an average of 68% with EFT (Church & Brooks, 2010). That's an impressive two-thirds drop. Now ask yourself, if EFT can produce a two-thirds drop in pain, why can't it produce a 100% drop? I pondered this question myself, and I asked many therapists and doctors for their theories as to why this might be so.

The consensus is that the two thirds of pain reduced by EFT is due largely to emotional causes, while the remaining one third of the pain has a physical derivation. A man I'll call "John" volunteered for a demonstration at an EFT introductory evening at which I presented. He was on crutches, and told us he had a broken leg as a result of a car accident. On a scale of 0 to 10, with 0 being no pain, and 10 being maximum pain, he rated his pain as an 8. The accident had occurred 2 weeks earlier. My logical scientific brain didn't think EFT would work for John, because his pain was purely physical. I tapped with him anyway. At the end of our session, which lasted less than 15 minutes, his pain was down to a 2. I hadn't tapped on the actual pain with John at all, but rather on all the emotional components of the auto accident.

There were many such components. His wife had urged him to drive to an event, but he didn't want to go and felt resentment toward his wife. That's emotional. He was angry at the driver of the other car. That's emotional. He was mad at himself for abandoning his own needs by driving to an event he didn't want to attend. That's emotional. He was upset that now, as an adult, he was reenacting the abandonment by his mother that he had experienced as a child. That's emotional. He was still hurt by an incident that occurred when he was 5 years old, when his mother was supposed to pick him up from a friend's birthday party and forgot because she was socializing with her friends and drinking. That's emotional.

Do you see the pattern here? We're working on a host of problems that are emotional, yet interwoven with the pain. The physical pain is overlaid with a matrix of emotional issues, like self-neglect, abandonment, anger, and frustration, which, in John's case, were part of the fabric of his life.

John's story has a happy ending. After we'd tapped on each of the emotional components of his pain, the physical pain in his broken leg went down to a 2. That pain rating revealed the extent of the physical component of John's problem. Two of the original eight rating points were physical. The other six points were emotional.

The same is true for the person who's afraid of public speaking, who has a spider phobia, who's suffering from a physical ailment, who's feeling trapped in his job, who's unhappy with her husband, who's in conflict with those around him. That is, all of these problems have a large component of unfinished emotional business from the past. When you neutralize the underlying emotional issues with EFT, what remains is the real problem, which is often far smaller than you imagine.

Though I present at few conferences nowadays because of other demands on my time, I used to present at about 30 medical and psychological conferences each year, speaking about research and teaching EFT. I presented to thousands of medical professionals during that period. One of my favorite sayings was "Don't medicalize emotional problems. And don't emotionalize medical problems." When I would say this to a roomful of physicians, they would nod their heads in unison. The medical profession as a whole is very aware of the emotional component of disease.

If you have a real medical problem, you need good medical care. No ifs, ands, or buts. If you have an emotional problem, you need EFT. Most problems are a mixture of both. That's why I urge you to work on the emotional component with EFT and other safe and non-invasive behavioral methods, and to get the best possible medical care for the physical component of your problem. Talk to your doctor about this; virtually every physician will be supportive of you bolstering your medical treatment with emotional catharsis.

When you feel better emotionally, a host of positive changes also occur in your energy system. When you feel worse, your energy system follows. Several researchers have hooked people up to electroencephalographs (EEGs), and taken EEG readings of the electrical energy in their brains before and after EFT. These studies show that when subjects are asked to recall a traumatic event, their patterns of brain-wave activity change. The brain-wave frequencies associated with stress, and activation of the fight-or-flight response, dominate their EEG readings. After successful treatment, the brain waves shown on their EEG readings are those that characterize relaxation (Lambrou, Pratt, & Chevalier, 2003; Swingle, Pulos, & Swingle, 2004; Diepold & Goldstein, 2008).

Other research has shown similar results from acupuncture (Vickers et al., 2012). The theory behind acupuncture is that our body's energy flows in 12 channels called meridians. When that energy is blocked, physical or psychological distress occurs. The use of acupuncture needles, or acupressure with the fingertips, is believed to release those energy blocks. EFT has you tap with your fingertips on the end points of those meridians; that's why EFT is sometimes referred to as "emotional acupuncture." When your energy is balanced and flowing, whether it's the brain-wave energy picked up by the EEG or the meridian energy described in acupuncture, you feel better. That's another reason why EFT works well for many different kinds of problem.

EFT is rooted in sound science, and this chapter is devoted to showing you how to do Clinical EFT yourself so you can enjoy some of the benefits research has demonstrated. It will introduce you to the basic concepts that amplify the power of EFT, and steer you clear of the most common pitfalls that prevent people from making progress with EFT. The basics of EFT, called the "Basic Recipe," are easy to learn and use. The second half of this chapter shows you how to apply the Basic Recipe for maximum effect and introduces you to all of the key concepts of Clinical EFT.

Testing

EFT doesn't just hope to be effective. We test our results constantly, to determine if the course we're taking is truly making us feel better. The basic scale we use for testing was developed by a famous psychiatrist, Joseph Wolpe, in the 1950s, and measures a person's degree of discomfort on a scale of 0 through 10. Zero indicates no discomfort, and 10 is the maximum possible distress. This scale works equally well for psychological problems such as anxiety and physical problems such as pain.

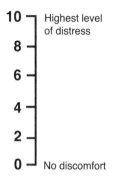

SUD scale (intensity meter)

Dr. Wolpe called this rating the SUD or Subjective Units of Discomfort. It's also sometimes called the Subjective Units of Distress scale. You feel your problem, and give it a number rating on the SUD scale. It's vital to rate your SUD level as it is *right now*, not imagine what it might have been at the time in the past when the problematic event occurred. If you can't quickly identify a number, just take your best guess, and go from there.

I recommend you write down your initial SUD number. It's also worth noting *where in your body* the information on your SUD level is coming from. If you're working on a physical pain such as a headache, where in your head is the ache centered? If you're working on a traumatic emotional event, perhaps a car accident, where in your body is your reference point for your emotional distress? Do you feel it in your belly, your heart, your forehead? Write down the location on which your SUD rating is based.

A variation of the numeric scale is a visual scale. If you're working with a child who does not yet know how to count, for example, you can ask the child to spread his or her hands apart to indicate how big the problem is. Wide-open arms mean big, and hands close together mean small.

Whatever methods you use for testing, each round of EFT tapping usually begins with this type of assessment of the size of the problem. This allows us to determine whether or not our approach is working. After we've tested and written down our SUD level and body location, we move on to EFT's Basic Recipe. It has this name to indicate that EFT consists of certain ingredients, and if you want to be successful, you need to include them, just as you need to include all the ingredients in a recipe for chocolate chip cookies if you want your end product to be tasty.

Many years ago, I published a book by Wally Amos. Wally is better known as "Famous Amos" for his brand of chocolate chip cookies. One day I asked Wally, "Where did you get your recipe?" I thought he was going to tell me how he'd experimented with hundreds of variations to find the best possible combination of ingredients. I imagined Wally like Thomas Edison in his laboratory, obsessively combining pinches of this and smidgeons of that, year after year, in order to perfect the flavor of his cookies, the way Edison tried thousands of combinations before discovering the incandescent light bulb.

Wally's offhand response was "I used the recipe on the back of a pack of Toll House chocolate chips." Toll

House is one of the most popular brands, selling millions of packages each year, and the simple recipe is available to everyone. I was astonished, and laughed at how different the reality was from my imaginary picture of Wally as Edison. Yet the message is simple: Don't reinvent the wheel. If it works, it works. Toll House is so popular because their recipe works. Clinical EFT produces such good results because the Basic Recipe works. While a master chef might be experienced enough to produce exquisite variations, a beginner can bake excellent cookies, and get consistently great results, just by following the basic recipe. This chapter is designed to provide you with that simple yet reliable level of knowledge.

EFT's Basic Recipe omits a procedure that was part of the earliest forms of EFT, called the 9 Gamut Procedure. Though the 9 Gamut Procedure has great value for certain conditions, it isn't always necessary, so we leave it out. The version of EFT that includes it is called the Full Basic Recipe (see Appendix A of *The EFT Manual*).

The Setup Statement

The Setup Statement systematically "sets up" the problem you want to work on. Think about arranging dominoes in a line in the game of creating a chain reaction. Before you start the game, you set them up. The object of the game is to knock them down, just as EFT expects to knock down your SUD level, but to start with, you set up the pieces of the problem.

The Setup Statement has its roots in two schools of psychology. One is called cognitive therapy, and the other is called exposure therapy. Cognitive therapy considers the large realm of your cognitions—your thoughts, beliefs, ways of relating to others, and the mental frames through which you perceive the world and your experiences.

Exposure therapy is a successful branch of psychotherapy that vividly exposes you to your negative experiences. Rather than avoiding them, you're confronted by them, with the goal of breaking your conditioned fear response to the event.

We won't go deeper into these two forms of therapy now, but you'll later see how EFT's Setup Statement draws from cognitive and exposure approaches to form a powerful combination with acupressure or tapping.

Psychological Reversal

The term "Psychological Reversal" is taken from energy therapies. It refers to the concept that when your energies are blocked or reversed, you develop symptoms. If you put the batteries into a flashlight backward, with the positive end where the negative should be, the light won't shine. The human body also has a polarity (see illustration). A reversal of normal polarity will block the flow of energy through the body. In acupuncture, the goal of treatment is to remove obstructions, and to allow the free flow of energy through the 12 meridians. If reversal occurs, it impedes the healing process.

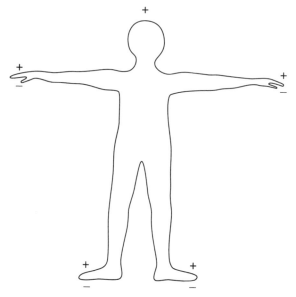

The human body's electrical polarity (adapted from
ACEP Certification Program Manual, 2006)

The way Psychological Reversal shows up in EFT and
other energy therapies is as a failure to make progress in
resolving the problem. It's especially prevalent in chronic
diseases, addictions, and conditions that resist healing. If
you run into a person who's desperate to recover, yet who
has had no success even with a wide variety of different
therapies, the chances are good that you're dealing with
Psychological Reversal. One of the first steps of EFT's
Basic Recipe is to correct for Psychological Reversal. It
only takes a few seconds, so we include this step whether
or not Psychological Reversal is present.

EFT's Setup includes stating an affirmation with those elements drawn from cognitive and exposure therapies, while at the same time correcting for Psychological Reversal.

Affirmation

The exposure part of the Setup Statement involves remembering the problem. You expose your mind repeatedly to the memory of the trauma. This is the opposite of what we normally do; we usually want an emotional trauma to fade away. We might engage in behaviors such as dissociation or avoidance so that we don't have to deal with unpleasant memories.

As you gain confidence with EFT, you'll find yourself becoming fearless when it comes to exposure. You'll discover you don't have to remain afraid of old traumatic memories; you have a tool that allows you to reduce their emotional intensity in minutes or even seconds. The usual pattern of running away from a problem is reversed. You feel confident running toward it, knowing that you'll quickly feel better.

The EFT Setup Statement is this:

Even though I have (name of problem), I deeply and completely accept myself.

You insert the name of the problem in the exposure half of the Setup Statement. Examples might be:

Even though I had that dreadful car crash, I deeply and completely accept myself.

Even though I have this migraine headache, I deeply and completely accept myself.

Even though I have this fear of heights, I deeply and completely accept myself.

Even though I have this pain in my knees, I deeply and completely accept myself.

Even though I had my buddy die in my arms in Iraq, I deeply and completely accept myself.

Even though I have this huge craving for whiskey, I deeply and completely accept myself.

Even though I have this fear of spiders, I deeply and completely accept myself.

Even though I have this urge to eat another cookie, I deeply and completely accept myself.

The list of variations is infinite. You can use this Setup Statement for anything that bothers you.

While exposure is represented by the first half of the Setup Statement, before the comma, cognitive work is done by the second half of the statement, the part that deals with self-acceptance. EFT doesn't try to induce you to positive thinking. You don't tell yourself that things will get better, or that you'll improve. You simply express the intention of accepting yourself just the way you are. You accept reality. Gestalt therapist Byron Katie (2002) wrote a book entitled *Loving What Is,* and that's exactly what EFT recommends you do.

The Serenity Prayer uses the same formula of acceptance, with the words, "God grant me the serenity to accept the things I cannot change; courage to change the things I can; and wisdom to know the difference." With EFT, you don't try and think positively. You don't try and change your attitude or circumstances; you simply affirm that you accept them. This cognitive frame of accepting what is opens the path to change in a profound way. It's also quite difficult to do this in our culture, which bombards us with positive thinking. Positive thinking actually gets in the way of healing in many cases, while acceptance provides us with a reality-based starting point congruent with our experience. The great 20th-century therapist Carl Rogers, who introduced client-centered therapy, said that the paradox of transformation is that change begins by accepting conditions exactly the way they are (Rogers, 1961).

I recommend that at first you use the Setup Statement exactly as I've taught it here. As you gain confidence, you can experiment with variations. The only requirement is that you include both a self-acceptance statement and exposure to the problem. For instance, you can invert the two halves of the formula, and put cognitive self-acceptance first, followed by exposure. Here are some examples:

I accept myself fully and completely, even with this miserable headache.

I deeply love myself, even though I have nightmares from that terrible car crash.

I hold myself in high esteem, even though I feel such pain from my divorce.

When you're doing EFT with children, you don't need an elaborate Setup Statement. You can have children use very simple self-acceptance phrases, like "I'm okay" or "I'm a great kid." Such a Setup Statement might look like this:

Even though Johnny hit me, I'm okay.

The teacher was mean to me, but I'm still an amazing kid.

You'll be surprised how quickly children respond to EFT. Their SUD levels usually drop so fast that adults have a difficult time accepting the shift. Although we haven't yet done the research to discover why children are so receptive to change, my hypothesis is that their behaviors haven't yet been cemented by years of conditioning. They've not yet woven a thick neural grid in their brains through repetitive thinking and behavior, so they can let go of negative emotions fast.

What do you do if your problem is self-acceptance itself? What if you believe you're unacceptable? What if you have low self-esteem, and the words "I deeply and completely accept myself" sound like a lie?

What EFT suggests you do in such a case is say the words anyway, even if you don't believe them. They will usually have some effect, even if at first you have difficulty with them. As you correct for Psychological Reversal in the way I will show you here, you will soon find yourself shifting from unbelief to belief that you are acceptable. You can say the affirmation aloud or silently. It carries more emotional energy if it is said emphatically or loudly, and imagined vividly.

Secondary Gain

While energy therapies use the term Psychological Reversal to indicate energy blocks to healing, there's an equivalent term drawn from psychology. That term is "secondary gain." It refers to the benefits of being sick. "Why would anyone want to be sick?" you might wonder. There are actually many reasons for keeping a mental or physical problem firmly in place.

Consider the case of a veteran with PTSD. He's suffering from flashbacks of scenes from Afghanistan where he witnessed death and suffering. He has nightmares, and never sleeps through the night. He's so disturbed that he cannot hold down a job or keep a relationship intact for long. Why would such a person not want to get better, considering the damage PTSD is doing to his life?

The reason might be that he's getting a disability check each month as a result of his condition. His income is dependent on having PTSD, and if he recovers, his main source of livelihood might disappear with it.

Another reason might be that he was deeply wounded by a divorce many years ago. He lost his house and children in the process. He's fearful of getting into another romantic relationship that is likely to end badly. PTSD gives him a reason to not try.

These are obvious examples of secondary gain. When we work with participants in EFT workshops, we uncover a wide variety of subtle reasons that stand in the way of healing. One woman had been trying to lose weight for 5 years and had failed at every diet she tried. Her secondary gain turned out to be freedom from unwanted attention by men.

Another woman, who suffered from fibromyalgia, discovered that her secret benefit from the disease was that she didn't have to visit relatives she didn't like. She had a ready excuse for avoiding social obligations. She also got sympathetic attention from her husband and children for her suffering. If she gave up her painful disease, she might lose a degree of affection from her family and have to resume seeing the relatives she detested.

Just like Psychological Reversal, secondary gain prevents us from making progress on our healing journey. Correcting for these hidden obstacles to success is one of the first elements in EFT's Basic Recipe.

How EFT Corrects for Psychological Reversal

The first tapping point we use in the EFT routine is the side of the hand (SH) point, located on the fleshy outer portion of the hand. EFT has you tap the SH point with the tips of the four fingers of the opposite hand.

Side of the hand (SH) point

Repeat your affirmation emphatically three times while tapping your side of the hand point. You've now corrected for Psychological Reversal, and set up your energy system for the next part of EFT's Basic Recipe, the Sequence.

The Sequence

Next, you tap on meridian end points in sequence. Tap firmly, but not harshly, with the tips of your first two fingers, about seven times on each point. The exact number is not important; it can be a few more or less than seven. You can tap on either the right or left side of your body, with either your dominant or nondominant hand.

First tap on the meridian endpoints found on the face (see illustration). These are: (1) at the start of the eyebrow, where it joins the bridge of the nose; (2) on the outside edge of the eye socket; (3) on the bony ridge of the eye socket under the pupil; (4) under the nose; and (5) between the lower lip and the chin.

Then tap (6) on one of the collarbone points (see illustration). To locate this point, place a finger in the notch between your collarbones. Move your finger down about an inch and you'll feel a hollow in your breastbone. Now move it to the side about an inch and you'll find a deep hollow below your collarbone. You've now located the collarbone acupressure point.

Finally, tap (7) on the under the arm point, which is about four inches below the armpit (for women, this is where a bra strap crosses).

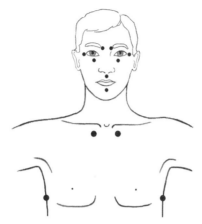

EB, SE, UE, UN, Ch, CB and UA points

The Reminder Phrase

Earlier, I emphasized the importance of exposure. Exposure therapy has been the subject of much research, which has shown that prolonged exposure to a problem, when coupled with techniques to calm the body, treats traumatic stress effectively. EFT incorporates exposure in the form of a Reminder Phrase. This is a brief phrase that keeps the problem at the front of your mind while you tap on the acupressure points. It keeps your energy system focused on the specific issue you're working on, rather than jumping to other thoughts and feelings. The aim of the Reminder Phrase is to bring the problem vividly into your experience, even though the emotionally triggering situation might not be present now.

For instance, if you have test anxiety, you use the Reminder Phrase to keep you focused on the fear, even though you aren't actually taking a test right now. That gives EFT an opportunity to shift the pattern in the absence of the real problem. You can also use EFT during an actual situation, such as when you're taking an actual test, but most of the time you're working on troublesome memories. The Reminder Phrase keeps you targeted on the problem. An example of a Reminder Phrase for test anxiety might be *"That test"* or *"The test I have to take tomorrow"* or *"That test I failed."* Other examples of Reminder Phrases are:

The bee sting

Dad hit me

Friend doesn't respect me

Lawyer's office

Sister told me I was fat

Car crash

This knee pain

Tap each point while repeating your Reminder Phrase. Then tune in to the problem again, and get a second SUD rating. The chances are good that your SUD score will now be much lower than it was before.

These instructions might seem complicated the first time you read them, but you'll soon find you're able to complete a round of EFT tapping from memory in 1 to 2 minutes.

Let's now summarize the steps of EFT's Basic Recipe:

1. Assess your SUD level.

2. Insert the name of your problem into the Setup Statement: *"Even though I have (this problem), I deeply and completely accept myself."*

3. Tap continuously on the side of the hand point while repeating the Setup Statement three times.

4. While repeating the Reminder Phrase, tap about seven times on the other seven points.

5. Test your results with a second SUD rating.

Isn't that simple? You now have a tool that, in just a minute or two, can effectively neutralize the emotional sting of old memories, as well as help you get through bad current situations. After a few rounds of tapping, you'll find you've effortlessly memorized the Basic Recipe, and you'll find yourself using it often in your daily life.

If Your SUD Level Doesn't Come Down to 0

Sometimes a single round of tapping brings your SUD score to 0. Sometimes it only brings it down slightly. Your migraine might have been an 8, and after a round of EFT it's a 4. In these cases, we do EFT again. You can adjust your affirmation to acknowledge that a portion of the problem sill remains, for example, *"Even though I still have some of this migraine, I deeply and completely accept myself."* Here are some further examples:

Even though I still feel some anger toward my friend for putting me down, I deeply and completely accept myself.

Even though I still have a little twinge of that knee pain, I deeply and completely accept myself.

Even though the bee sting still smarts slightly, I deeply and completely accept myself.

Even though I'm still harboring some resentment toward my boss, I deeply and completely accept myself.

Even though I'm still somewhat frustrated with my daughter for breaking her agreement, I deeply and completely accept myself.

Even though I'm still upset when I think of being shipped to Iraq, I deeply and completely accept myself.

Adjust the Reminder Phrase accordingly, as in *"some anger still"* or *"remaining frustration"* or *"bit of pain"* or *"somewhat upset."*

EFT for You and Others

You can do EFT on yourself, as you've experienced during these practice rounds. You can also tap on others. Many therapists, life coaches, and other practitioners offer EFT professionally to clients. I'm far more inclined to have clients tap on themselves during EFT sessions, even in the course of a therapy or coaching session. Though the coach can tap on the client, having clients tap on themselves, with some guidance by the coach, puts the power squarely in the clients' hands. Clients are empowered by discovering that they are able to reduce their own emotional distress, and they leave the practitioner's office with a self-help tool at their fingertips any time they need it. In some jurisdictions, it is illegal or unethical for therapists to touch clients at all, and EFT when done only by the client is still effective in these cases.

The Importance of Targeting Specific Events

During EFT workshops, I sometimes write on the board:

The Three Most Important Things About EFT

Then, under that, I write:

Specific Events
Specific Events
Specific Events

It's my way of driving home the point that a focus on specific events is critical to success in EFT. In order to release old patterns of emotion and behavior, it's vital to identify and correct the specific events that gave rise to those problems. When you hear people say, "I tried EFT and it didn't work," the chances are good that they were tapping on generalities, instead of specifics.

An example of a generality is "self-esteem" or "depression" or "performance problems." These aren't specific events. Beneath these generalities is a collection of specific events. The person with low self-esteem might have been coloring a picture at the age of 4 when her mother walked in and criticized her for drawing outside the lines. She might have had another experience of a schoolteacher scolding her for playing with her hair during class in second grade, and a third experience of her first boyfriend deciding to ask another girl to the school dance. Together, those specific events contributed to the global pattern of low self-esteem. The way EFT works is that when the emotional trauma of those individual events is resolved, the whole pattern of low self-esteem can shift. If you tap on the big pattern, and omit the specific events, you're likely to have limited success.

When you think about how a big pattern like low self-esteem is established, this makes sense. It's built up through many single events. Collectively, they form the whole pattern. The big pattern doesn't spring to life fully formed; it's built gradually out of many similar experiences. The memories engraved in your brain are of individual events; one disappointing or traumatic memory at a time is encoded in your memory bank. When enough similar memories have accumulated, their commonalities combine to create a common theme like "poor self-esteem." Yet the theme originated as a series of specific events, and that's where EFT can be effectively applied.

You don't have to use EFT on every single event that contributed to the global theme. Usually, once a few of the most disturbing memories have lost their emotional impact, the whole pattern disappears. Memories that are similar lose their impact once the most vivid memories have been neutralized with EFT.

Tapping on global issues is the single most common mistake newcomers make with EFT. Using lists of tapping phrases from a website or a book, or tapping on generalities, is far less effective than tuning in to the events that contributed to your global problem, and tapping on them. If you hear someone say, "EFT doesn't work," the chances are good they've been tapping globally rather than identifying specific events. Don't make this elementary mistake. List the events, one after the other, that stand out most vividly in your mind when you think about the global problem. Tap on each of them, and you'll usually find the global problem diminishing of its own accord. This is called the "generalization effect," and it's one of the key concepts in EFT.

Tapping on Aspects

EFT breaks traumatic events and other problems into smaller pieces called "aspects." The reason for this is that the highest emotional charge is typically found in one small chunk of the event, rather than the entirety of the event. You might need to identify several different aspects, and tap on each of them, before the intensity of the whole event is reduced to a 0.

Here's an example of tapping on aspects, drawn from experience at an EFT workshop I taught. A woman in her late 30s volunteered as a subject. She'd had neck pain and limited range of motion since an automobile accident 6 years before. She could turn her head to the right most of the way but had only a few degrees of movement to the left. The accident had been a minor one, and why she still suffered 6 years later was something of a mystery to her.

I asked her to feel where in her body she felt the most intensity when recalling the accident, and she said it was in her upper chest. I then asked her about the first time she'd ever felt that way, and she said it was when she'd been involved in another auto accident at the age of 8. Her sister had been driving the car. We worked on each aspect of the early accident. The two girls had hit another car head on at low speed while driving around a bend on a country road. One emotionally triggering aspect was the moment she realized that a collision was unavoidable, and we tapped till that lost its force. We tapped on the sound of the crash, another aspect. She had been taken to a neighbor's house, bleeding from a cut on her head, and we tapped on that. We tapped on aspect after aspect. Still, her pain level didn't go down much, and her range of motion didn't improve.

Then she gasped and said, "I just remembered. My sister was only 15 years old. She was underage. That day, I dared her to drive the family car, and we totaled it." Her guilt turned out to be the aspect that held the most emotional charge, and after we tapped on that, her pain disappeared, and she regained full range of motion in her neck. If we'd tapped on the later accident, or failed to uncover all the aspects, we might have thought, "EFT doesn't work."

Aspects can be pains, physical sensations, emotions, images, sounds, tastes, odors, fragments of an event, or beliefs. Make sure you dig deep for all the emotional charge held in each aspect of an event before you move on to the next one. One way of doing this is to check each sensory channel, and ask, "What did you hear/see/taste/touch/smell?" For one person, the burned-rubber smell of skidding tires might be the most terrifying aspect of a car accident. For another, it might be the smell of blood. Yet another person might remember most vividly the sound of the crash or the screams. For another person, the maximum emotional charge might be held in the feeling of terror at the moment of realization that the crash was inevitable. The pain itself might be an aspect. Guilt, or any other emotion, can be an aspect. For traumatic events, it's necessary to tap on each aspect.

Thorough exploration of all the aspects will usually yield a complete neutralization of the memory. If there's still some emotional charge left, the chances are good that you've missed an aspect, so go back and find out what shards of trauma might still be stuck in place.

Finding Core Issues

One of my favorite sayings during EFT workshops is "The problem is never the problem." What I mean by this is that the problem we complain about today usually bothers us only because it resembles an earlier problem. For example, if your spouse being late disturbs you, you may discover by digging deep with EFT that the real reason this behavior triggers you is that your mother didn't meet your needs in early childhood. Your spouse's behavior in the present day resembles, to your brain, the neglect you experienced in early childhood, so you react accordingly. You put a lot of energy into trying to change your spouse when the present-day person is not the source of the problem.

On the EFT Universe website, we have published hundreds of stories in which someone was no longer triggered by a present problem after the emotional charge was removed from a similar childhood event. Nothing changed in the present day, yet the very problem that so vexed a person before now carries zero emotional charge. That's the magic that happens once we neutralize core issues with EFT. Rather than being content with using EFT on surface problems, it's worth developing the skills to find and resolve the core issues that are at the root of the problem.

Here are some questions you might ask in order to identify core issues:

- Does the problem that's bothering you remind you of any events in your childhood? Tune in to your body and feel your feelings. Then travel back in time to the first time in your life you ever felt that same sensation.

- What's the worst similar experience you ever had?

- If you were writing your autobiography, what chapter would you prefer to delete, as though it had never happened to you?

If you can't remember a specific childhood event, simply make up a fictional event in your mind. This kind of guessing usually turns out to be right on target. You're assembling the imagined event out of components of real events, and the imaginary event usually leads back to actual events you can tap on. Even if it doesn't, and you tap on the fictional event, you will usually experience an obvious release of tension.

The Generalization Effect

The generalization effect is a phenomenon you'll notice as you make progress with EFT. As you resolve the emotional sting of specific events, other events with a similar emotional signature also decrease in intensity. I once worked with a man at an EFT workshop whose father had beaten him many times during his childhood. His SUD level on the beatings was a 10. I asked him to recall the worst beating he'd ever suffered. He told me that when he was 8 years old, his father had hit him so hard he had broken the boy's jaw. We tapped together on that terrible beating, and after working on all the aspects, his SUD score dropped to a 0. I asked him for a SUD rating on all the beatings, and his face softened. He said, "My dad got beat by his dad much worse than he beat me. My dad actually did a pretty good job considering how badly he was raised." My client's SUD level on all the beatings dropped considerably after we reduced the intensity of this one beating. That's an example of EFT's generalization effect. When you knock down an important domino, all the other dominoes can fall.

This is very reassuring to clients who suffered from many instances of childhood abuse, the way my client at that workshop had suffered. You don't need to work through every single horrible incident. Often, simply collapsing the emotional intensity behind one incident is sufficient to collapse the intensity around similar incidents.

The reason our brains work this way is because of a group of neurons in the emotional center of the brain (the limbic system) called the hippocampus. The hippocampus has the job of comparing one event to the other. Suppose that, as a 5-year-old child in Catholic school, you were beaten by a nun. Forty years later, you can't figure out why you feel uneasy around women wearing outfits that are black and white. The reason for your adult aversion to a black-and-white combination is that the hippocampus associates the colors of the nun's habit with the pain of the beating.

This was a brilliant evolutionary innovation for your ancestors. Perhaps these early humans were attacked by a tiger hiding in the long grass. The tiger's stripes mimicked the patterns of the grass, yet there was something different there. Learning to spot a pattern, judge the differences, and react with fear saved your alert ancestors. They gave birth to their children, who also learned, just a little bit better, how to respond to threats. After thousands of generations, you have a hippocampus at the center of your brain that is genetically engineered to evaluate every message flooding in from your senses, and pick out those associated with the possibility of danger. You see the woman wearing the black-and-white cocktail dress at a party, your hippocampus associates these colors with the nun who beat you, and you have an emotional response.

Yet the opposite is also true. Assume for a moment you're a man who is very shy when confronted with women at cocktail parties. He feels a rush of fear whenever he thinks about talking to an attractive woman dressed in black. He works with an EFT coach on his memories of getting beaten by the nun in Catholic school, and suddenly he finds himself able to talk easily to women at parties. Once the man's hippocampus breaks the connection between beatings and a black dress, it knows, for future reference, that the two phenomena are no longer connected. This is the explanation the latest brain science gives us for the generalization effect (Phelps & LeDoux,

2005). It's been noted in EFT for many years, and it's very comforting for those who've suffered many adverse experiences. You may need to tap on some of them, but you won't have to tap on all of them before the whole group is neutralized. Sometimes, like my client who was beaten repeatedly as a child, if you tap on a big one, the generalization effect reduces the emotional intensity of all similar experiences.

The Movie Technique and Tell the Story Technique

When you take an EFT workshop, the first key technique you learn is the Movie Technique. Why do we place such emphasis on the Movie Technique? The reason is that it combines many of the methods that are key to success with EFT.

The first thing the Movie Technique does is focus you on being specific. EFT is great at eliminating the emotional intensity you feel, as long as it's used on an actual concrete event ("John yelled at me in the meeting") rather than a general statement ("My procrastination").

The Movie Technique has you identify a particular incident that has a big emotional charge for you, and systematically reduce that charge to 0. You picture the event in your mind's eye as though it were a movie, and run through the movie scene by scene.

Whenever you reach a part of the movie that carries a big emotional charge, you stop and perform the EFT sequence. In this way, you reduce the intensity of each of the bad parts of the movie. EFT's related technique, Tell the Story, is done out loud, while the Movie Technique is typically done silently. You can use the Movie Technique with a client without the client ever disclosing what the event was.

Try this with one of your own traumatic life events right now. Think of the event as though it were a scary movie. Make sure it's an event that lasts just a few minutes; if your movie lasts several hours or days, you've probably picked a general pattern. Try again, selecting a different event, till you have a movie that's just a few minutes long.

One example is a man whose general issue is "Distrust of Strangers." We traced it to a particular childhood incident that occurred when the man, whom we'll call David, was 7 years old. His parents moved to a new town, and David found himself walking to a new school through a rough neighborhood. He encountered a group of bullies at school but always managed to avoid them. One day, walking back from school, he saw the bullies walking toward him. He crossed the street, hoping to avoid their attention. He wasn't successful, and he saw them point at him, then change course to intercept him. He knew he was due for a beating. They taunted him and shoved him, and he fell into the gutter. His mouth hit the pavement, and he chipped a tooth. Other kids gathered round and laughed at him, and the bullies moved off. He picked himself up and walked the rest of the way home.

If you were to apply EFT to David's general pattern, "Distrust of Strangers," you'd be tapping generally—and ineffectually. When instead you focus on the specific event, you're homing in on the life events that gave rise to the general pattern. A collection of events like David's beating can combine to create the general pattern.

Now give your movie a title. David might call his movie "The Bullies."

Start thinking about the movie at a point before the traumatic part began. For David, that would be when he was walking home from school, unaware of the events in store for him.

Now run your movie through your mind till the end. The end of the movie is usually a place where the bad events are over. For David, this might be when he picked himself up off the ground, and resumed his walk home.

Now let's add EFT to your movie. Here's the way you do this:

1. Think of the title of your movie. Rate the degree of your emotional distress around just the title, not the movie itself. For instance, on the distress scale of 0 to 10, where 0 is no distress and 10 represents maximum distress, you might be an 8 when you think of the title "The Meeting." Write down your movie title, and your number.

2. Work the movie title into an EFT Setup Statement. It might sound something like this: *"Even though I experienced [insert your movie title here], I deeply and completely accept myself."* Then tap on the EFT acupressure points, while repeating the Setup Statement three times. Your distress level will typically go down. You may have to do EFT several times on the title for it to reach a low number, 0 or 1 or 2.

3. Once the title reaches a low number, think of the "neutral point" before the bad events in the movie began to take place. For David, the neutral point was when he was walking home from school, before the bullies saw him. Once you've identified the neutral point of your own movie, start running the movie through your mind, until you reach a point where the emotional intensity rises. In David's case, the first emotionally intense point was when he saw the bullies.

4. Stop at this point, and assess your intensity number. It might have risen from a 1 to a 7, for instance. Then perform a round of EFT on that first emotional crescendo. For David, it might be, *"Even though I saw the bullies turn toward me, I deeply and completely accept myself."* Use the same kind of statement for your own problem: *"Even though [first emotional crescendo], I deeply and completely accept myself."* Keep tapping till your number drops to 0 or near 0, perhaps a 1 or 2.

5. Now rewind your mental movie to the neutral point, and start running it in your mind again. Stop at the first emotional crescendo. If you sail right through the first one you tapped on, you know you've really and truly resolved that aspect of the memory with EFT. Go on to the next crescendo. For David, this might have been when the bullies shoved him into the gutter. When you've found your second emotional crescendo, then repeat the process: Assess your intensity number, do EFT, and keep tapping till your num-

ber is low. Even if your number is only a 3 or 4, stop and do EFT again. Don't push through low-intensity emotional crescendos; since you have the gift of freedom at your fingertips, use it on each part of the movie.

6. Rewind to the neutral point again, and repeat the process.

7. When you can replay the whole movie in your mind, from the neutral point to the end of the movie when your feelings are neutral again, without feeling an emotional charge, you'll know you've resolved the whole event. You'll have dealt with all the aspects of the traumatic incident.

8. To truly test yourself, run through the movie but exaggerate each sensory channel. Imagine the sights, sounds, smells, tastes, and other aspects of the movie as vividly as you possibly can. If you've been running the movie silently in your mind, speak it out loud. When you cannot possibly make yourself upset, you're sure to have resolved the lingering emotional impact of the event. The effect is usually permanent.

When you work through enough individual movies in this way, the whole general pattern often vanishes. Perhaps David had 40 events that contributed to his distrust of strangers. He might need to do the Movie Technique on all 40, but experience with EFT suggests that when you resolve just a few key events, perhaps 5 or 10 of them, the rest fade in intensity, and the general pattern itself is neutralized.

The Tell the Story Technique is similar to the Movie Technique; as mentioned, the Movie Technique is usually performed silently while Tell the Story is out loud. One great benefit of the Movie Technique done silently is that the client does not have to disclose the nature of the problem. An event might be too triggering, too embarrassing, or too emotionally overwhelming to be spoken aloud. That's no problem with the Movie Technique, which allows EFT to work its magic without the necessity of disclosure on the part of the client. The privacy offered by the Movie Technique makes it very useful for clients who would rather not talk openly about troubling events.

Constricted Breathing

Here's a way to demonstrate how EFT can affect you physically. You can try this yourself right now. It's often practiced as an onstage demonstration at EFT workshops. You simply take three deep breaths, stretching your lungs as far as they can expand. On the third breath, rate the extent of the expansion of your lungs on a 0-to-10 scale, with 0 being as constricted as possible, and 10 being as expanded as possible. Now perform several rounds of EFT using Setup Statements such as:

Even though my breathing is constricted...

Even though my lungs will only expand to an 8...

Even though I have this physical problem that prevents me breathing deeply...

Now take another deep breath and rate your level of expansion. Usually, there's substantial improvement.

Now focus on any emotional contributors to constricted breathing. Use questions like:

- What life events can I associate with breathing problems?

- Are there places in my life where I feel restricted?

- If I simply guess at an emotional reason for my constricted breathing, what might it be?

Now tap on any issues surfaced by these questions. After your intensity is reduced, take another deep breath and rate how far your lungs are now expanding. Even if you were a 10 earlier, you might now find you're an 11 or 14.

The Personal Peace Procedure

The Personal Peace Procedure consists of listing every specific troublesome event in your life and systematically using EFT to tap away the emotional impact of these events. With due diligence, you knock over every negative domino on your emotional playing board and, in so doing, remove significant sources of both emotional and physical ailments. You experience personal peace, which improves your work and home relationships, your health, and every other area of your life.

Tapping on large numbers of events one by one might seem like a daunting task, but we'll show you in the next few paragraphs how you can accomplish it quickly and efficiently. Because of EFT's generalization effect, where tapping on one issue reduces the intensity of similar issues, you'll typically find the process going much faster than you imagined.

Removing the emotional charge from your specific events results in less and less internal conflict. Less internal conflict results, in turn, in greater personal peace and less suffering on all levels—physical, mental, emotional, and spiritual. For many people, the Personal Peace Procedure has led to the complete cessation of lifelong issues that other methods did not resolve. You'll find stories on the EFT Universe website written by people who describe relief from physical maladies such as headaches, breathing difficulties, and digestive disorders. You'll read other stories of people who used EFT to help them deal with the stress associated with AIDS, multiple sclerosis, and cancer. Unresolved anger, trauma, guilt, or grief contributes to physical illness, and cannot be medicated away. EFT addresses these emotional contributors to physical disease.

Here's how to do the Personal Peace Procedure:

1. List every specific troublesome event in your life that you can remember. Write them down in a Personal Peace Procedure journal. "Troublesome" means it caused you some form of discomfort. If you listed fewer than 50 events, try harder to remember more. Many people find hundreds. Some bad events you recall may not seem to cause you any current discomfort. List them anyway. The fact that they came to mind suggests they may need resolution. As you list them, give each specific event a title, like it's a short movie, such as: Mom slapped me that time in the car; I stole my brother's baseball cap; I slipped and fell

in front of everybody at the ice skating rink; My third-grade class ridiculed me when I gave that speech; Dad locked me in the toolshed overnight; Mrs. Simmons told me I was dumb.

2. When your list is finished, choose the biggest dominoes on your board, that is, the events that have the most emotional charge for you. Apply EFT to them, one at a time, until the SUD level for each event is 0. You might find yourself laughing about an event that used to bring you to tears; you might find a memory fading. Pay attention to any aspects that arise and treat them as separate dominoes, by tapping for each aspect separately. Make sure you tap on each event until it is resolved. If you find yourself unable to rate the intensity of a bad event on the 0-to-10 scale, you might be dissociating, or repressing a memory. One solution to this problem is to tap 10 rounds of EFT on every aspect of the event you are able to recall. You might then find the event emerging into clearer focus but without the same high degree of emotional charge.

3. After you have removed the biggest dominoes, pick the next biggest, and work on down the line.

4. If you can, clear at least one of your specific events, preferably three, daily for 3 months. By taking only minutes per day, in 3 months you will have cleared 90 to 270 specific events. You will likely discover that your body feels better, that your threshold for getting upset is much lower,

your relationships have improved, and many of your old issues have disappeared. If you revisit specific events you wrote down in your Personal Peace Procedure journal, you will likely discover that their former intensity has evaporated. Pay attention to improvements in your blood pressure, pulse, and respiratory capacity. EFT often produces subtle but measurable changes in your health, and you may miss them if you aren't looking for them.

5. After knocking down all your dominoes, you may feel so much better that you're tempted to alter the dosages of medications your doctor has prescribed. Never make any such changes without consulting your physician. Your doctor is your partner in your healing journey. Tell your doctor that you're working on your emotional issues with EFT, as most health care professionals are acutely aware of the contribution that stress makes to disease.

The Personal Peace Procedure does not take the place of EFT training, nor does it take the place of assistance from a qualified EFT practitioner. It is an excellent supplement to EFT workshops and help from EFT practitioners. EFT's resources are designed to work in combination for the most effective healing results.

Is It Working Yet?

Sometimes EFT's benefits are blindingly obvious. In the introductory video on the home page of the EFT

Universe website, you see a TV reporter with a lifelong fear of spiders receiving a tapping session. Afterward, in a dramatic turnaround, she's able to stroke a giant hairy tarantula spider she's holding in the palm of her hand.

Other times, EFT's effects are subtler and you have to pay close attention to spot them. A friend of mine who has had a lifelong fear of driving in high-speed traffic remarked to me recently that her old fear is completely gone. Over the past year, each time she felt anxious about driving, she pulled her car to the side of the road and tapped. It took many trips and much tapping, but subtle changes gradually took effect. Thanks to EFT, she has emotional freedom and drives without fear. She also has another great benefit, in the form of a closer bond with her daughter and baby granddaughter. They live a 2-hour drive away and, previously, her dread of traffic kept her from visiting them. Now she's able to make the drive with joyful anticipation of playing with her granddaughter.

If you seem not to be making progress on a particular problem despite using EFT, look for other positive changes that might be happening in your life. Stress affects every system in the body, and once you relieve it with EFT, you might find improvements in unexpected areas. For instance, when stressed, the capillaries in your digestive system constrict, impeding digestion. Many people with digestive problems report improvement after EFT. Stress also redistributes biological resources away from your reproductive system. You'll find many stories on EFT Universe of people whose sex lives improved dramatically as a by-product of healing emotional issues.

Stress affects your muscular and circulatory systems; many people report that muscle aches and pains disappear after EFT, and their blood circulation improves. Just as stress is pervasive, relaxation is pervasive, and when with EFT we release our emotional bonds, the relaxing effects are felt all over the body. So perhaps your sore knee has only improved slightly, but you're sleeping better, having fewer respiratory problems, and getting along better with your coworkers.

Saying the Right Words

A common misconception is that you have to say just the right words while tapping in order for EFT to be effective. The truth is that focusing on the problem is more important than the exact words you're using. It's the exposure to the troubling issue that directs healing energy to the right place; the words are just a guide.

Many practitioners write down tapping scripts with lists of affirmations you can use. These can be useful. However, your own words are usually able to capture the full intensity of your emotions in a way that is not possible using other people's words. The way you form language is associated with the configuration of the neural network in your brain. You want the neural pathways along which stress signals travel to be very active while you tap. Using your own wording is more likely to awaken that neural pathway fully than using even the most eloquent wording suggested by someone else. By all means, use tapping scripts if they're available, to nudge you in the right direction. At the same time, utilize the power of prolonged exposure by focusing your mind completely on your own experience. Your mind and body have a healing wisdom that usually directs healing power toward the place where it is most urgently required.

The Next Steps on Your EFT Journey

Now that you've entered the world of EFT, you'll find it to be a rich and supportive place. On the EFT Universe website, you'll find stories written by thousands of people, from all over the world, describing success with an enormous variety of problems. Locate success stories on your particular problem by using the site's drop-down menu, which lists issues alphabetically: Addictions, ADHD, Anxiety, Depression, and so on. Read these stories for insights on how to apply EFT to your particular case. They'll inspire you in your quest for full healing.

Our certified practitioners are a wonderful resource. They've gone through rigorous training in Clinical EFT and have honed their skills with many clients. Many of them work via telephone or videoconferencing, so if you don't find the perfect practitioner in your geographic area, you can still get expert help with remote sessions. Though EFT is primarily a self-help tool and you can get great results alone, you'll find the insight that comes from an outside observer can often alert you to behavior patterns and solutions you can't find by yourself.

Take an EFT workshop. EFT Universe offers more than a 100 workshops each year, all over the world, and you're likely to find Level 1 and 2 workshops close to you. You'll make friends, see expert demonstrations, and learn

EFT systematically. Each workshop contains eight learning modules, and each module builds on the one before. Fifteen years' experience in training thousands of people in EFT has shown us exactly how people learn EFT competently and quickly, and provided the background knowledge to design these trainings. Read the many testimonials on the website to see how deeply transformational the EFT workshops are.

The EFT Universe newsletter is the medium that keeps the whole EFT world connected. Read the stories published there weekly to stay inspired and to learn about new uses for EFT. Write your own experiences and submit them to the newsletter. Post comments on the EFT Universe Facebook page, and comment on the blogs.

If you'd like to help others access the benefits you have gained from EFT, you might consider volunteering your services. There are dozens of ways to support EFT's growth and progress. You can join a tapping circle, or start one yourself. You can donate to EFT research and humanitarian efforts. You can offer tapping sessions to suffering people through one of EFT's humanitarian projects, like those that have reached thousands in Haiti, Rwanda, and elsewhere. You can let your friends know about EFT.

EFT has reached millions of people worldwide with its healing magic but is still in its infancy. By reading this book and practicing this work, you're joining a healing revolution that has the potential to radically reduce human suffering. Imagine if the benefits you've already experienced could be shared by every child, every sick person, every anxious or stressed person in the world. The trajectory of human history would be very different. I'm committed to helping create this shift however I can, and I invite you to join me and all the other people of goodwill in making this vision of a transformed future a reality.

References

Church, D., & Brooks, A. J. (2010). The effect of a brief EFT (Emotional Freedom Techniques) self-intervention on anxiety, depression, pain and cravings in healthcare workers. *Integrative Medicine: A Clinician's Journal, 9*(4), 40–44.

Diepold, J. H., & Goldstein, D. (2008). Thought Field Therapy and qEEG changes in the treatment of trauma: A case study. *Traumatology, 15*(1), 85–93. http://dx.doi.org/10.1177/1534765608325304

Katie, Byron. (2002). *Loving what is: Four questions that can change your life.* New York, NY: Harmony Books.

Lambrou, P. T., Pratt, G. J., & Chevalier, G. (2003). Physiological and psychological effects of a mind/body therapy on claustrophobia. *Subtle Energies and Energy Medicine, 14,* 239–251.

Phelps, E. A., & LeDoux, J. E. (2005). Contributions of the amygdala to emotion processing: From animal models to human behavior. *Neuron, 48,* 175–187.

Rogers, C. R. (1961). *On becoming a person: A therapist's view of psychotherapy.* New York, NY: Houghton Mifflin.

Swingle, P. G., Pulos, L., & Swingle, M. K. (2004). Neurophysiological indicators of EFT treatment of post-traumatic stress. *Subtle Energies and Energy Medicine, 15*(1), 75–86.

Vickers, A. J., Cronin, A. M., Maschino, A. C., Lewith, G., MacPherson, H., Foster, N. E.,…Linde, K. (2012, October 22). Acupuncture for chronic pain: Individual patient data meta-analysis. *Archives of Internal Medicine, 172*(19), 1444–1453. doi:10.1001/archinternmed. 2012.3654

3

The Science of Meditation: Benefits and Brain Waves

People start to meditate for various reasons, ranging from stress to headaches and other physical ailments, to inability to focus and concentrate, to wanting more peace and calmness in life, to wanting a deeper spiritual connection. While the reasons for starting a practice vary, we derive benefits on all levels from meditation, whether we're looking for them or not.

The Health and Well-Being Benefits of Meditation

Psychologists in the mid 20th century undertook a scientific examination of meditation (Shapiro, 1980). These studies first dealt with how meditation could be used as a quality adjunct to psychotherapeutic intervention. This was also an era that began the study of meditation as a tool for self-regulation. Shapiro (1990) argued that the effort to determine the effects of meditation on health and well-being fits easily in the realm of psychotherapy research, noting that the problem was setting up effective protocols to be able to study meditation accurately.

Clinical psychologist and noted EFT practitioner Patricia Carrington, PhD, cites the following improvements associated with meditation: reduction in tension-anxiety, improvement in stress-related illnesses, increased productivity, decrease in addictive behavior, reduced self-blame, lowered irritability, and mood elevation, among other benefits (Carrington, 1990). Ajaya (1977) noted that meditation and modalities related to meditation were being used for the treatment of stress, drug dependency, tension headaches, anxiety, and a variety of other psychogenic (having a psychological origin) disorders.

As soon as we start to meditate, we experience the therapeutic benefits. With meditation practice, we learn to pay attention to all levels of our being—body, breath, emotions, mind, and subtler experiences that may be difficult to express in words. Meditators experience a tranquil state of mind, which helps the immune system by limiting its reaction to stress and strain. Over time, meditation decreases the amount of sleep we need and energizes both body and mind. Our mood improves and we view the world with a more positive outlook and less anxiety.

One study explored the effects of a mindfulness meditation–based stress reduction program on mood disturbance and symptoms of stress in cancer patients (Speca, Carlson, Goodey, & Angen, 2000). A randomized, wait-list controlled design was used on 90 patients with a mean age of 51 years and different types and stages of cancer. Patients were randomly assigned to either an immediate treatment group or a wait-list control group. All patients completed the Profile of Mood States and the Symptoms of Stress Inventory both before and after the intervention. The intervention included a weekly meditation group (1.5 hours) for seven weeks plus home meditation practice.

After the intervention, patients in the treatment group had significantly lower scores on Total Mood Disturbance and also had fewer overall symptoms of stress; fewer cardiopulmonary and gastrointestinal symptoms; less emotional irritability, depression, and cognitive disorganization; and fewer habitual patterns of stress. There was a 65% overall reduction in total mood disturbance and a 31% reduction in symptoms of stress.

Another study explored the effects of meditation on depression, as measured by the Beck Depression Questionnaire, and cardiac health, as measured by blood pressure and heart rate (Delui, Yari, Khouyinezhad, Amini, & Bayazi, 2013). Forty-five patients with cardiovascular disease and depression were randomly assigned to three groups: relaxation, meditation, or control. Patient age, gender, literacy level, and marital status were matched among the groups.

The Beck Depression scale and a self-assessment of anxiety were completed. Ten sessions in physical muscle relaxation or mindfulness meditation were compared to no intervention. Significant reductions in depression scores, systolic blood pressure, and heart rate were seen in the meditation group as compared with the control group. There was no significant difference in blood pressure, heart rate, or depression between the relaxation and control groups, although the authors noted that other studies have resulted in significant changes using relaxation techniques.

Meditation helps us tap into all the capacities of the mind—memory, concentration, emotion, and reasoning—and also helps us tap into intuition. As we continue practicing, we have a better grasp of how to enhance these capacities and use them to their fullest potential.

In a study by Hall (1999), the academic performance of African-American college students who meditated was compared to a control group of non-meditators. Fifty-six undergraduates enrolled in a Hampton University introduction to psychology course were randomly assigned to meditation and non-meditation groups. A one-factor analysis of variance was done on the data for the fall 1994 cumulative grade point averages (GPAs), which determined that the two groups were evenly matched at the start of the experiment. The first group was instructed in the use of a simple meditation method involving breathing, relaxation, and focusing techniques. Both groups attended one-hour study sessions twice a week. The meditation group practiced meditation for 10 minutes at the beginning and 10 minutes at the end of each study session. They were also asked to use this technique when studying at home and before they took tests. The control group attended the study groups with no other intervention.

The results indicated that the semester GPAs of the meditation group were significantly higher than the control group. In addition, their cumulative GPAs were also significantly higher. The conclusion was drawn that if the students could learn more in a semester, they could also learn more in a year, as well as in their entire academic career. Though it was indicated that further research is needed, these findings were considered a good start in finding a way to help students improve their academic performance using meditation.

In a preliminary study by Newberg, Wintering, Khalsa, Roggenkamp, and Waldman (2010), 14 subjects with memory problems underwent an eight-week meditation program to determine if there were any significant changes in memory and cerebral blood flow (CBF). The subjects had an IV inserted and were injected with 250MBq of tC-99m ECD (a radiation dose) while listening to a neutral stimulus CD. The subjects then had a pre-program baseline SPECT scan (a nuclear imaging test that shows how an organ works). They were then guided through a meditation session on a CD, received an injection of 925MBq ECD, and had a pre-program meditation scan. The subjects then went through the eight-week meditation program with the same scanning protocol that resulted in a post-program baseline and meditation scan. The results indicated that there were significant increases in baseline CBF ratios in the prefrontal, superior frontal, and superior parietal cortices. Improvements after meditation training were noted in neuropsychological test scores of verbal fluency, Trails B (a test of visual attention and task-switching ability), and logical memory. The researchers noted the need for further testing, with more subjects.

Another study explored both brain function and immune function in 25 healthy employees in their work environment (Davidson et al., 2003). An eight-week training program in mindfulness meditation was used in a randomized, controlled study. Brain electrical activity was measured before and immediately after, and then four months after the eight-week meditation-training program. At the end of the eight-week period, subjects in both groups were vaccinated with influenza vaccine.

Increases in the activation of the left front side of the prefrontal cortex were reported in meditators compared with the non-meditators. This pattern suggests a decrease in anxiety and negative affect (display of emotions or feelings) and an increase in positive affect. The meditation subjects also showed significant increases in antibody titers (the amount and diversity of antibodies that correlate to the strength of the body's immune response) to influenza vaccine compared with those in the wait-list control group. The researcher's findings suggest that brain and immune function may be changed in positive ways with the practice of meditation (Davidson et al., 2003).

Meditation works on health from the inside out. Many modern diseases can be classified as psychosomatic, meaning that the body becomes imbalanced and prone to disease due to our thoughts and emotions. We can take a drug or even a natural remedy to alleviate illness and the symptoms might decrease or go away, but if the same emotional or mental pattern remains that caused the illness in the first place, the illness is likely to return. The underlying cause still needs to be addressed. With meditation, we become our own therapists, exploring the consequences of particular emotional responses and thought patterns. As we realize and change these patterns, the outcomes of these patterns spontaneously change.

Meditation provides a means to manage stress. With practice, we have less anxiety and experience more positive emotions. We become less reactive as we slowly work through the issues and challenges that used to trigger emotional responses. We may note this in various ways such as: not reacting to a difficult coworker, getting along better with family members, being less fearful of being judged, venturing to try new things, or changing our self-talk so we're not so hard on ourselves.

In one study, loving-kindness meditation was shown to increase the frequency of positive emotions, with the consequential buildup of personal resources (Fredrickson, Cohn, Coffey, Pek, & Finkel, 2008). Half of the 139 working adult subjects were randomly assigned to a loving-kindness meditation group and the others were assigned to a control group. The subjects in the meditation group showed increases over time in daily experiences of positive emotions. This, in turn, produced increases in a wide range of personal resources, including increased mindfulness, purpose in life, and social support as well as a decrease in illness symptoms. As these personal resources increased, there was also an increase in life satisfaction and reduced depressive symptoms.

* * *

EcoMeditation

By Dawson Church, PhD

I developed a technique called EcoMeditation (EcoMeditation.com). It combines EFT tapping, neuro-feedback, heart coherence, and mindfulness in a seven-step routine. The routine uses simple physiological instructions such as "Relax your tongue on the floor of your mouth."

These physiological steps provide cues to the body. Each cue triggers a type of relaxation. One induces heart coherence, another induces an alpha state, while yet another relaxes the autonomic nervous system. The result is that, in less than four minutes, even failed meditators are able to enter the same deeply relaxed state that it usually takes years of practice for a meditator to experience.

When hooking people up to EEG machines while they practice EcoMeditation, we see marked changes in their brain function. Their alpha waves expand in amplitude, while beta waves shrink. Theta and delta waves balance out. After a few minutes, gamma waves appear and stabilize, indicating coordination between the many different parts of the brain.

EcoMeditation is an example of a practice that we can do to deliberately induce high amplitudes of alpha, the brain wave typical of peak performance. At the beginning of an EcoMeditation workshop, it takes people in the group about four minutes to enter this peak state, but by the end of the weekend, only 90 seconds. They leave with the ability to induce this mental state at will.

In one live workshop, I taught EcoMeditation to Prem, a 42-year-old man with moderate anxiety. He was a computer programmer who wanted to bring more creativity into his life. Prem played the guitar, but rarely made time for this, his favorite hobby. "I just don't have time for myself," he said. One of his core beliefs was, "Life is tough. You have to apply yourself. There's no time for play."

At the beginning of our session, Prem's EEG showed a high degree of beta waves in both the left and right hemispheres of his brain. Beta is the signature wave of stress. His alpha waves were minimal. Alpha is the idea state, one of relaxed alertness. It's in the middle of the frequency band, and connects the higher frequencies of beta and gamma with the lower frequencies of theta and delta. People in highly creative states, as well as healers, show high amplitudes of theta and delta.

Prem's EEG readout showed plenty of theta and delta, but his minimal alpha amplitude was like a bottleneck; he didn't have access to his creative side. His high amplitude of beta is also characteristic of people with chronic anxiety, stress, and burnout (Fehmi & Robbins, 2007).

EcoMeditation uses EFT tapping to clear obstacles to relaxation. It then takes you through a series of simple physical relaxation exercises that send signals of safety to the brain and body. It does not rely on belief or philosophy; instead, it's based on sending the body physiological cues that produce a deeply relaxed state automatically.

Once Prem settled into the EcoMeditation routine, he had big flares of alpha in both the right and left hemispheres of his brain, though larger on the right. His anxious stressed-out beta waves disappeared. His brain began to produce gamma waves, which it had not been doing before. Gamma is the highest frequency and is typical of brains making connections between all the different brain lobes. Gamma helps synchronize the different parts of the brain to work together.

Though Prem was not a meditator and said that he had taken meditation classes but never succeeded in establishing a routine meditation practice, EcoMeditation quickly settled him into a deep state. His brain waves stabilized in an ideal pattern called the Awakened Mind.

This brain-wave pattern is characterized by large amplitudes of alpha, theta, and delta in both the left and right hemispheres of the brain. Anxious beta frequencies are minimal, while gamma expands. Despite Prem's previous inability to meditate, he was able to attain an Awakened Mind brain-wave pattern using the simple Energy Psychology techniques that are part of EcoMeditation. In the absence of stress, the blood rushed back into his prefrontal cortex and his thinking became clear as he gained access to the biological and intellectual assets in the executive centers of his brain.

At that workshop, we tested the biological responses of participants as well as their psychological states before and after the workshop. Prem's set point for cortisol, the primary stress hormone, dropped from a high of 6.72 to 5.43 nMol/L. When our stress levels drop, biological resources are freed up for cell repair, immunity, and other beneficial functions.

This was evident in Prem's levels of salivary immuno-globulin A (SigA), a key immune marker. They rose from 32.55 to 39.3 ug/ml between the beginning and the end of the workshop. His resting heart rate dropped from 79 to 64 beats per minute (BPM), while his blood pressure dropped from 118/80 to 108/70.

Similar positive effects were noted for other work-shop participants. For the whole group, average cortisol levels declined from 7.50 to 5.30 nMol/L. SigA levels rose from 216.78 to 275.06 ug/ml. Resting heart rate dropped from 70 to 66 (Groesbeck et al., 2016).

Once we reversed the stress response with EcoMeditation, Prem began to see the light side of life. The blood began to flow back into his forebrain and his whole hard drive came back online. He felt empowered. He knew he had resources. He knew he had the capacity for play. He regained a sense of control in his life. He had a sense of agency, of self-efficacy, and his whole story changed as a result of a simple and brief Energy Psychology practice.

Such techniques reverse the emotional overwhelm and degraded brain function that occurs when people are stressed. They regain access to all the abilities and resources in their thinking brain: memory, rational thought, practices that foster resiliency, and the ability to be objective.

❊ ❊ ❊

Meditation helps us develop keen focus and concentration. The skills we hone in meditation carry over into our daily lives, enabling us to prioritize more easily what needs to be done, do tasks in less time and with greater effectiveness, solve problems, and engage our creativity. Our capacity to do work increases, and we may find ourselves taking on projects that we would never have considered attempting before we began to meditate.

Meditation helps us explore our inner realms, those parts of ourselves that are nonphysical but whose existence we intuit. This level goes beyond the mind. The experiences of mystics, spiritual leaders, saints, and sages reflect these realms. We are equipped to have similar experiences. Many of us have already had experiences that have opened the door into these realms and we would like to know how to get back there at will. Meditation is a way to do that.

Because deep meditation experiences are of a nonphysical nature and beyond words, scientists have tried to make headway into this realm by studying consciousness from the perspective of brain-wave and neural activity. While the brain is a physical organ and not a true reflection of an ultimate state of consciousness, per the adepts, this scientific model is nonetheless a worthwhile starting point.

The Scientific and Mystical Models

In their groundbreaking work *The Awakened Mind*, Cade and Coxhead (1989) explain that a standard assumption of science is the psychoneural identity thesis. This thesis posits that consciousness is based in the chemical and electrical activity of the brain, thereby making consciousness dependent on brain activity.

Quantum physicists have addressed this matter. Dr. Amit Goswami (2008) explains a difference between downward causation and upward causation and implicates what he calls consciousness or quantum consciousness in this distinction. Goswami associates the psychoneural identity thesis with upward causation. The implication of this is that matter is the origin of everything. On the other hand, the experience of the subjective scientists, the adepts, and now quantum physics is that consciousness or quantum consciousness is the substratum for all that exists, the ground of all being. This they call downward causation. Goswami explains that our scientific materialist paradigm observes only things external to the body, objectivity being its primary perspective.

Meditation and related practices are a subjective science—the exploration of the internal world, the internal universe of an individual. The outcomes associated with meditation are replicable, however. That is, given the proper experimental protocol, any sincere person can succeed in verifying subjectively what those before them have verified.

It is clear that there are differing perspectives in the scientific community regarding the underlying causes of consciousness. There are similar differences of opinion regarding meditation and the mystics. The findings of quantum physics and neurotheology (the study of what part of the brain is triggered during mystical experiences) may be bringing the observations of the mystics and meditation out of the realm of pseudoscience.

An example of the controversy regarding the mystics' findings beyond the realm of the physical is evident in the historical record of religion. Mystic theology and dogmatic theology have often been at odds, along similar lines as the differences between quantum physics and the psychoneural identity paradigm. Here is an example.

In the 14th century, a mystic named Gregory debated with a dogmatist regarding his (Gregory's) direct experience. Gregory defended the position that he and his students experienced an uncreated light as they progressed in their practice. These "navel psychics," as his antagonist disparagingly referred to Gregory and his followers, used their breath to control the mind and a repetitive word or phrase to refine their concentration. In time, they claimed to experience this uncreated light, which they equated with deification (theosis) or union with divine energies that are eternal, supernatural, and uncreated (Palmer, Sherrard, & Ware, 1995). The debate here seems to be between direct personal experience and intellectual/book knowledge. The debate rages on to this day.

Brain versus Mind

Are the brain and the mind the same thing? What is the mind? Masters often pose such questions to their meditation students. The truth of the matter is that we want to understand ourselves, but we don't understand some of the basic processes of our being. Meditation comes in here as a tool to help us increase the subtlety of our awareness and provide for us a basic experiential understanding of these processes.

The Western scientific model views the process of thinking as the by-product of electrical and chemical reactions in the brain; thereby, we have an existence. The mind, being equated with the physical structure known as the brain, functions because of these activities.

To the adepts, the mind is thoughts, thoughts are the mind. One meditation master, Swami Rama, went so far as to say that "all the body is in the mind, but all the mind is not in the body," implying that the brain (the physical body) and the mind are somehow different. One of the statements often heard from beginning meditators is that they want to stop the mind, or focus the mind, when, in point of fact, they are unsure of what this thing called mind is or where it's located. Based on what is known about the mind, the knowledge that is commonly accepted, we are under the illusion (per the adepts) that we have no control over our emotional health, no control over our physical health, and certainly no control over our evolution as human beings.

To give you an idea of how your mind and senses actually relate to each other, consider the following. As you read these words, is it the words on the page of the book, computer, or Kindle screen that are coming and grasping your sense of sight or is it that your sense of seeing goes out to grasp what is before your eyes? Which is it? Remember our earlier observation about momentarily not seeing or hearing during a lecture or other public event? If you think about that example and the questions you just considered here, the conclusion seems to be that the mind is necessary for the perception through the senses to happen.

The adepts observed that the mind directs the senses of sight, hearing, smell, taste, and touch to go out and experience the world. (Did you, prior to this, understand or consider this relationship? If so, you are the exception.) The mind withholding the senses is how sense withdrawal takes place as a choice. We make a choice to change the focus of our senses, the directional habit of the senses. Granted, for the beginner, sense withdrawal may be easier said than done because the relationship of the mind to the senses is not understood experientially. Yet it might be easier than you think. As you experiment with meditation, you can test and verify the adepts' observations about the senses and the mind.

Based on our simple definition of meditation ("...a family of techniques which have in common a conscious attempt to focus attention in a nonanalytical way, and an attempt not to dwell on discursive, ruminating thought"— with senses withdrawn), let's consider some things that are often compared to meditation in the common experience. Listening to music is often considered meditation. As is said, "Music has charms to soothe the savage beast." Is the soothing itself meditation? Some people consider the practice of yoga and tai chi to be meditation. These practices are definitely used to calm the physical body and mind. Are these things really meditation? Meditation, in the ultimate sense, is more than being relaxed.

Meditation versus Hypnosis

Is there a difference between hypnosis and meditation? First let's consider how the definitions of hypnosis are similar and different from our proposed definition of meditation. Clark Hull, a famous researcher and author of *Hypnosis and Suggestibility*, defined hypnosis as "a state of relatively heightened susceptibility to prestige suggestion" (Baker, 1990). Dave Elman, who trained physicians to use hypnosis, defined it as "a state of mind in which the critical faculty of the human is bypassed, and selective thinking established" (Elman, 1964). Milton Erickson, renowned psychiatrist and foremost proponent of hypnosis, was quoted as saying hypnosis is "concentrating on your thoughts, values, memories and beliefs about life" (Baker, 1990).

Meditation does not involve suggestion, which is inherent to traditional hypnosis. Meditation, per our simple definition, is specifically an "attempt to focus attention in a nonanalytical way, and an attempt not to dwell on discursive, ruminating thought."

Another way of comparing hypnosis and meditation is to consider the brain-wave activity present in each. From the Mind Mirror EEG protocol introduced by Cade and Coxhead (1989) to the current 64 pin EEG and neuroscience technology of today, we know that our brain-wave activity ranges from gamma waves to beta, alpha, theta, and delta (Davidson & Lutz, 2008; Kaufman, 2005). Gamma waves are high frequency waves at approximately 40-100 Hertz (cycles per second). Beta waves are 12-40 Hertz, alpha 8-12 Hertz, theta 4-8 Hertz, and delta 1-4 Hertz. (The precise numbers vary slightly across sources, but these are the general ranges.)

Relating the states of waking, dreaming, and deep dreamless sleep specifically to one set of brain-wave activity is an oversimplification, but it serves our purpose here. From readings on early EEG technology, West (1990) placed meditation and the hypnogogic state (related to hypnosis) at the theta frequency. The mind-mirror EEG technology of Cade and Coxhead (1989, p. 117) suggested the following:

- Waking state: beta

- Hypnogogic state (the state between waking and dream): alpha

- Dreaming state: theta

- Deep dreamless sleep state: delta

- Meditative state: alpha and theta

- Highest meditative state: beta, alpha, theta, and delta

If Cade and Coxhead's findings are accurate, they show a difference between the states of meditation and hypnosis. In Cade and Coxhead's paradigm, the brain is much more active during the hypnogogic state than during the meditative or dreaming sleep state. It is important to note that hypnosis can bring about the relaxation response. As stated, an obvious difference between hypnosis and meditation is suggestion. In meditation, if the senses are withdrawn, external suggestion would not be registered. There are those who would say that the repetitive use of a word or words in the relaxation response paradigm (developed by Harvard physician Herbert Benson, 1975), the repetitive use of words or phrases of the Hesychast tradition (Eastern Orthodox mysticism) or a mantra in other traditions is the same as the autosuggestion of hypnosis. The adepts disagree. The ultimate state, the supramundane, transcends suggestion.

The idea here is that the end results of hypnosis and meditation are different, even though there is some debate about how close or not close the brain-wave activity of each state is to the other. As any good hypnotist knows, all hypnosis is self-hypnosis, meaning that hypnosis, the state, is brought on by oneself. When one knows how to enter the state, one can use it. The goal of meditation is transcendence. Should hypnosis touch this territory, it is no longer hypnosis in the sense that hypnosis is usually defined.

Meditation as Conscious Dreaming

Meditation and dreaming have something in common. In dreams, there is a flow of ideas, whole movies that play in the mind. Researchers have noted the deep brain structures associated with dreaming (Hoss & Hoss, 2010). During dreaming, the limbic system, the emotional brain, remains active. We respond emotionally to our dreams.

Whether we are adherents of Freud's idea of dreams working out our wish fulfillment, Jung's building on that with his findings that dreams bring forth primordial archetypes from our unconscious to help resolve things, or some other theory, we watch our dreams. Basically, we watch our mind while being unaware of external events. Dream research reveals that our response to dealing with physical and psychological threats in dreams is the same stress response as occurs in waking-state stress events (Hoss & Hoss, 2010).

One approach to meditation is simply watching the thoughts that pass through the mind-field. We watch the flow of ideas or whole movies just as we do while dreaming, with the difference that meditation is done with full awareness and dreaming is not, with the exception of lucid dreaming, which is dreaming while being aware that one is dreaming.

In normal dreaming, we are at the mercy of the unconscious content. In the dream, we react—positively, negatively, or neutrally. The adepts' approach to meditation teaches that the content of the mind-field should be observed with no emotional response. This is not the experience of the average dreamer because there is no control over the response to content that comes up from the unconscious.

Meditation could be considered a practice of conscious dreaming, which is different from lucid dreaming in that it is not occurring in the sleep state. The same type of content that could create a nightmare can bubble up from the unconscious and interfere with meditation also, however. The physical and psychological responses that arise during dreaming are the same as during meditation (Hoss & Hoss, 2010). Something can frighten us in a dream and we respond physically and mentally. The same response can occur in meditation. This is something that often prevents beginners from continuing the practice of meditation. It often takes considerable time for the meditator to overcome the upsetting aspects of what arises. Overcoming emotional disturbance is a major work in the practice of meditation, learning the objective observer perspective, the disassociated perspective, on what comes up in the mind.

The adepts hint that dreaming is unnecessary if our life is completely balanced. The only sleep required is the time that we spend in deep dreamless sleep, three hours, per the adepts. There has been no definitive research to back up this contention, but there are numerous instances of people requiring considerably less than eight hours' sleep.

Researchers witnessed one adept, Swami Rama, go straight to deep dreamless sleep (remain there for 25 minutes), no dreaming, and return to full waking consciousness, all the while being fully aware of his surroundings. The dreamless sleep state was indicated by 0-3 Hertz brain waves (delta) and Rama's gentle snoring (Rama, Ballentine, & Ajaya, 1976).

Another interesting example of the brain of an adept meditator was observed by Dean Radin, PhD, of the Institute of Noetic Sciences in his research work with Swami Veda Bharati. In preparation for a research protocol, Dr. Radin observed that Swami Veda was interacting with him all the while the swami's brain-wave activity was that of a person in deep dreamless sleep (Parker, Bharati, & Fernandez, 2013). The measure of cycles per second for deep dreamless sleep are considered a given by the scientific community. Some say 0-3 cycles per second (Rama et al., 1976) indicate deep dreamless sleep and others say 1-4 cycles per second. Measurements may vary, but scientists agree that individuals in deep dreamless sleep are unaware of their surroundings, which the average person verifies every night. It does not take a scientific study to see that something unusual is occurring when a person whose brain registers deep dreamless sleep is in conversation with the external world. Based on such observations, some have posited that an individual abiding in this self-existent reality would have no discernable electrical activity in the brain when measured by EEG (Parker, Bharati, & Fernandez, 2013; Cade & Coxhead, 1989).

It should be obvious that, from the mundane perspective, meditation is hard to classify. One reason, the adepts say, is that we are using the mind to try to understand reality, the substratum. Whether we consider brain waves or how the brain looks when in the state of meditation, the reality is still beyond this, according to the adepts.

4

The Mind and the Breath in Meditation

There is no neurotic individual who is capable of exhaling in one breath, deeply and evenly.

—Wilhelm Reich, psychoanalyst and disciple of Sigmund Freud

The misconception that meditation is simply relaxation has led to the health benefits (the mundane aspects) of meditation being confused with the supramundane aspects of meditation. Science has come to understand the mundane aspects of meditation more fully after observing not only adepts, but also less experienced meditators who demonstrate the ability to control at least some portion of their autonomic nervous system (ANS). We can better understand these possible abilities by looking at how the ANS functions with respect to the breath.

The central nervous system (CNS) is divided into a conscious portion and a less than conscious portion. (Note that we use the terminology "less than conscious" because the masters explain that a human being is capable of controlling things in the body once considered completely unconscious.) The conscious portion of the CNS is that portion that uses your muscles to reach for and hold this book or the Kindle or other device with which you are reading this. The less than conscious portion, known as the autonomic nervous system, has two divisions (Figure 1).

The parasympathetic branch of the ANS stimulates the digestive juices and digestion, slows the heartbeat, constricts the bronchi, constricts pupil dilation, contracts the bladder, and controls relaxing the smooth muscles of the blood vessels, among other functions.

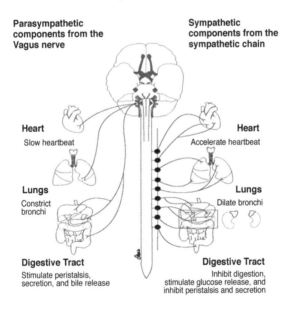

Parasympathetic components from the Vagus nerve

Sympathetic components from the sympathetic chain

Heart
Slow heartbeat

Heart
Accelerate heartbeat

Lungs
Constrict bronchi

Lungs
Dilate bronchi

Digestive Tract
Stimulate peristalsis, secretion, and bile release

Digestive Tract
Inhibit digestion, stimulate glucose release, and inhibit peristalsis and secretion

Figure 1. The two branches of the autonomic nervous system (partial): parasympathetic and sympathetic.
© 2017, Jennifer Hollis, MS, www.hollisvisualizations.com

The sympathetic branch mobilizes the body in the fight-or-flight response, which includes slowing unneeded functions such as digestion. Thus when danger is perceived, the sympathetic branch inhibits the digestive juices and digestion, speeds the heartbeat, dilates the pupils, inhibits bladder contraction, dilates the bronchi (for greater oxygen need), releases glycogen (fuel to burn), tenses muscles in preparation for use in fleeing or fighting danger, and stimulates the release of stress hormones such as cortisol.

The Mind Follows the Breath

Meditation masters have shown that the ANS can be made fully conscious. Breathing is one of those things that can be both conscious and less than conscious. There is an axiom related to the breath: *The breath follows the mind, and the mind follows the breath.* This means that the breath can be a starting point for understanding the mind. When the breath is deep, diaphragmatic, even, smooth, continuous, and quiet, the mind will naturally also be quiet. This type of breath regulation sets the stage for the meditator to go deeper without being disturbed by a racing mind. Such breath regulation is a standard for most novice meditators and a means by which meditation, as the adepts see it, can be gauged. By whatever means the meditative state is reached, there are specific qualities of the breath that will be present.

If you doubt the validity of the axiom "The breath follows the mind, and the mind follows the breath," consider the last time you were really angry. How was your breath affected? Now recall the last time you were totally at peace and happy, and compare that condition of the breath with the condition of your breath when you were angry.

To continue our understanding, we can make a couple of observations that don't require any electronic devices or much effort to monitor. The foundation for any mindfulness-based stress reduction starts with a simple awareness of the body. Many people resist such awareness, however. A physician who worked with patients on mindfulness-based stress-reduction techniques remarked to us, "People just don't want to take responsibility for themselves in an area where they can."

Part of the reason that people resist involves the connection between the body and mind. When tension is released in the body, the cause of the tension may begin to surface. If unpleasant memories and emotions are connected with the tension, then the person becomes aware of them and needs to process them in some way. If the person does not (consciously or unconsciously) feel able to deal with what arises, then resistance is a natural response. EFT can help here.

The body-mind connection is not taught in Western schools. We are not taught to be aware of ourselves. Thus many of us lack awareness of the benefits of self-knowledge. An ancient text suggests that the deity hampered our senses by making us turn to the external. The wise, the ancients would say, turn their attention inward. In this day and age, when we know so much about the psychogenic origins of disease, we all should become wise!

In the words of the Buddha, one of the world's great proponents of meditation, "It is easy to do what is wrong, to do what is bad for oneself; but very difficult to do what is right, to do what is good for oneself" (Mascaro, 1973, p. 58).

Another interesting aspect of resistance related to lack of awareness is the inability to digest or register the effects of an intervention based on self-regulation, as is evident in the Apex Effect in EFT. The Apex Effect refers to the phenomenon of experiencing a benefit from EFT but not being able to relate it to the EFT intervention.

Exercise: Observing the Breath

There are a few easy parameters you can observe to learn more about yourself through conscious breathing.

For these observations, you might want to lie on your back on the floor or other flat surface, with your feet spread at least a foot apart, and your arms alongside your body with the palms up. If this position bothers your lower back, you can place a rolled-up blanket beneath your knees, or bend your knees and put the soles of your feet on the floor. Or you can sit in a comfortable upright chair.

1. Let your arms rest on the floor 8 to 10 inches from the sides of your body with your shoulders down and away from your ears (or hands resting in your lap if you are seated).

2. Turn your hands so the palms are facing up, or at least set this intention (hand position is irrelevant

if you are in a chair). Make sure your head is comfortable; if you are lying on the floor, you may require a small cushion under your head for neck and shoulder comfort.

3. After you have situated yourself, close your eyes and begin to notice your breath and its qualities. Can you hear yourself breathe? (Note that conditions such as asthma or structural considerations in the nose such as a deviated septum will create more sound.)

4. As you lie or sit there, how is the breath flowing in and out of your body? Is it flowing smoothly or in a wavering, raggedy fashion?

5. As you are paying attention to your breath, consider the length of your exhalation compared to the length of your inhalation. Is there any noticeable difference in their length?

6. Does the breath stop at any point in the breathing cycle?

7. Notice how your body feels after having consciously brought your breathing into awareness. How has your body, how has your mind responded to this exercise? After making these observations, notice one more thing.

8. Note the movement or lack thereof in your abdomen as you breathe. (This movement or lack thereof will be of special significance when we later consider diaphragmatic breathing.)

9. Conclude these observations by simply letting your awareness externalize; do this by opening your eyes. You might find it useful to make a recording of this exercise, and go through these steps repeatedly.

Note: The authors offer free breath awareness, relaxation, and meditation downloads (see the website section of the appendix).

Let's now look individually at each of the aspects of the breath.

Noise in the Breath

The sources of noise in one's breathing can be many. As noted, a deviated septum or respiratory ailments such as asthma or the common cold can create more noise in the breath. One source of noise that is touchy for some people to consider is the noise produced by excess mucus associated with a poor diet. Poor dietary habits can hinder success with meditation, something we will address later. Excess mucus can be cleansed from the nostrils through a nasal wash using a neti pot or other method. If a person is serious about meditation, that person's habits and lifestyle will start to change.

Noise associated with breathing can come from something as practical and healthy as a good aerobic workout. The sympathetic branch of the autonomic nervous system is aroused during such exercise. The breathing rate increases and the breath becomes audible. Conversely, when we are calm, our breathing rate is slower and probably quiet, unless we have a respiratory or other condition.

Smooth or Irregular Breath

What might cause the breath to flow in and out of the body in a way that is not smooth and serene? One cause is surgery in which muscles were cut, which can result in an imbalance in the musculature, causing the breath to be jerky or raggedy as it flows in and out. A large majority of the muscles in the torso are involved in the breathing process, from the diaphragm, which we will discuss later, to the intercostal muscles between the ribs and more. The muscles working in a harmonious way is conducive to smooth breathing.

State of mind is another factor. The breathing of experienced meditators is different from the breathing of those who have not learned to self-induce a state of calm. A trained individual's breathing pattern tends to look like the sine curve in Figure 2.

Figure 2. A trained individual's breathing pattern depicted as a sine curve.

Comparing the pattern in Figure 2 to the one in Figure 3 and remembering the axiom "The mind follows the breath, the breath follows the mind," which mind would you prefer to have? Comparing the two breathing patterns, which would you think might be more conducive to balance and harmony for the body and the mind?

Figure 3. Irregular breathing pattern.

Research suggests a relationship between breathing and mental states. For example, hyperventilation has been associated with anxiety, panic disorder, migraine headaches, and other psychophysiological disorders (Fried & Golden, 1989). Our current understanding of psychogenic disorders such as hypertension has shown that relaxation, with its associated calming of the breath, can reverse such conditions.

Herbert Benson's observations are key here. He demonstrated the relationship between relaxation and health in *The Relaxation Response* (1975) and *Beyond the Relaxation Response* (1984). Nobel laureate Walter Hess laid the groundwork for Benson by mapping the relationship between the internal organs and certain brain centers, most notably the hypothalamus. In 1957, Hess's research led him to cite the following specific physiological parameters of the relaxation response (Cade & Coxhead, 1989):

1. Decrease in oxygen consumption
2. Reduction in carbon monoxide elimination
3. Reduction in:
   a. Heart rate
   b. Respiratory rate
   c. Blood pressure
   d. Muscle tone
   e. Blood cortisol levels
4. Increase in fingertip temperature
5. Increase in perfusion of internal organs

The relaxation response is important to our overall discussion because it will help us differentiate between a relaxation response and the ultimate potential of meditation.

Even or Uneven Length of Inhalation and Exhalation

In Figures 2 and 3, the peaks are the culmination of inhalation and the lows are the depth of an exhalation. Figure 2 represents a breathing pattern that is somewhat symmetrical with respect to the length of the inhalation and the exhalation, a pattern that the doctors Jerry indicate as ideal (Jerry, Jerry, & Bharati, 2007). In contrast, Figure 3 depicts irregularities in the length of inhalation and exhalation.

What our scientific medical paradigm knows is that there is a slight increase in the speed of our heart as we inhale and a slight decrease as we exhale. This is called sinus arrhythmia. You can observe this right where you sit. All you need do is to find a pulse point; most obvious is the carotid artery at the neck or the pulse at the wrist. Once you find this pulse, just sit quietly and breathe. Notice what happens to the pulse at the inception of your inhalation, and notice what happens at the inception of your exhalation.

When we inhale, we stimulate that portion of the ANS related to arousal. When we exhale, we stimulate that portion related to calming. In other words, when you felt your pulse increase, you were noting the stimulation of the sympathetic branch of your ANS. When you noticed the slight decrease in pulse rate, you were witnessing the stimulation of the parasympathetic branch. The adepts were aware of these relationships.

There are exceptions to this observation of the pulse. If you are a regular patterned breather, say a long distance runner or a lap swimmer, the sinus arrhythmia may not be apparent. Such individuals will have a heart rate relatively untouched by the inhalation and exhalation, due to their training. Likewise, a meditator might experience this as a side effect of working intensely with the breath.

Benson proposed four elements necessary for the relaxation response to occur. The first element is that there needs to be some mental device, a verbal or visual relaxation technique, to shift a person's state from a logical, external orientation to an internal imaging or receptive mode. The second element is that the person needs to assume a passive attitude, maintaining attention on the sense awareness exercises under way. The third and fourth elements pertain to the immediate environment of the individual; the person needs to be reasonably comfortable in posture and there should be a quiet atmosphere (Cade & Coxhead, 1989).

These elements draw our attention to the learning process of human beings. We get information from the environment; we learn from the environment through our senses. We all learn in a preferred way, and we key more predominantly on one or another of the sensory pathways. Considering Benson's first element in this light, a person with a tendency to be visual might prefer a visual rather than a verbal relaxation technique. The person with an auditory tendency might prefer the verbal relaxation approach.

The masters were aware of objects of meditation to fit the needs of every sensory pathway. Some theorists suggest that practices such as tai chi, qigong, the whirling of the Sufi dervishes, and the physical aspects of yoga fit the bill of providing a kinesthetic segue to altered states. The authors of *Sports, Energy, and Consciousness* would likely agree with this assessment of the kinesthetic aspect of transcendence (Leskowitz, 2014). The point is that there is a means for all interested, whatever their habit of learning, to approach the practice of meditation.

Benson's second element required for relaxation, the need for a passive or receptive attitude, may be difficult to achieve. In the authors' experience in training people in biofeedback, getting a person to assume a passive attitude, that is, a receptive attitude, is difficult. Most people have no idea what a passive or receptive attitude is, and words used to express how to accomplish it often confound the situation. Progress can be more rapid by having individuals pay attention to the qualities of the breath, gently guiding their awareness inward to the mostly unknown universe of their internal workings. This can be a daunting journey in itself, depending on the person, but it is an effective way to help someone achieve the physiological correlates of a passive, receptive attitude. Research on EFT has proven that just a brief period of tapping can bring about a more relaxed state and thus a more receptive attitude (Feinstein, 2008).

What we learn about the breath can be effective and practical knowledge for managing stress. Hans Selye, who built upon Nobel laureate Hess's findings, related his understanding of stress in terms of the fight-flight response (Selye, 1978). Later research by Stanford scientist Sapolsky (1994) added the phenomenon of freeze to the physiological responses to stress. In a discussion on posttraumatic stress disorder, Carol Look addresses the freeze response by explaining that it is related to a painful event being locked in the muscles of the body (Church, 2015). We posit that the adepts understood such phenomena and established paradigms of physical culture with a deep awareness of the breath, such as yoga, tai chi, or qigong, to address these types of issues.

Inherent to the development of EFT is the understanding that Dr. George Goodheart gained from traditional Chinese medicine. The major muscles of the body are related to internal organs (Thie & Thie, 2005). Related to the freeze response, for example, the emotion of fear could be expressed in the raised and held shoulders, raised shoulders being a clear sign of a startle response. Among the muscles associated with this response are the upper trapezius muscles; and the internal organs related to the upper trapezius are the kidneys. Emotions related to the kidneys are fear, anxiety, and awe, per traditional Chinese medicine. The collarbone tapping points in a regular EFT routine address the kidney meridian. If the upper trapezius muscles are locked in a raised position, EFT could help to remove this freeze response in the shoulders. The body was holding the emotion; clearing the body can clear the emotion. This bodily response is similar to what Look verified in her work with posttraumatic stress disorder clients and addressing the freeze response. The adepts would say that all of us are affected in some way by symptoms of posttraumatic stress disorder (PTSD) and relate this to our emotionally imbalanced lives.

The adepts can help us understand stress from a different perspective than that of the Western scientific paradigm. We can come to understand the adept perspective in the laboratory of our own bodies. A person who breathes evenly, that is, the inhalation and exhalation are equal, is showing a balanced ANS, a nervous system that is in homeostasis (Figure 4).

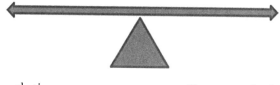

Sympathetic
   (Inhalation)

Parasympathetic
   (Exhalation)

Figure 4. The autonomic nervous system in homeostasis. The horizontal line on the fulcrum represents balance between the sympathetic and parasympathetic branches.

A nervous system impacted by the events of the day may momentarily (the key word here is "momentarily") lose homeostasis. This loss of homeostasis alone is not the stressor per se. Stressful life events are always going to happen. The real stressor is our not returning to homeostasis.

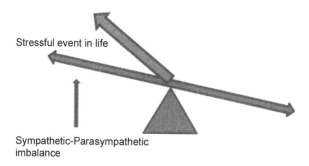

Figure 5. Autonomic nervous system imbalance.

Figure 5 depicts the nervous system state of a person whose less than conscious habit is maintaining a low level of sympathetic nervous system arousal all the time (the vertical blue arrow). The less than conscious habit of this person is an ANS that is out of balance, lacking homeostasis. After a stressful life event, depicted here by the red arrow, there is not a return to true homeostasis, a balanced ANS, but a continuation of the status quo, a chronically overstimulated sympathetic branch of the ANS (represented by the long blue line on the fulcrum).

In other cases, the imbalance tips to the parasympathetic side, with overstimulation of that branch of the ANS. The relationship between the ANS and health is an often-overlooked aspect of managing stress and psychogenic disease. The adepts' experience indicates that having a harmonious breathing pattern and thus a balanced ANS is key to health and success in meditation.

Pauses in the Breath

A pause in the breath is a curious consideration, given that an adept fully immersed in the meditative state may not have a perceptible breath. The adepts teach that a conscious pause in the breath is fine, but having habitual large unconscious pauses in the breath is less than healthy. Rama, Ballentine, and Hymes (1979) address this topic in *Science of Breath: A Practical Guide*, citing the example of the deadly pause of sleep apnea, with its nearly one-to-one correlation with heart disease. The authors proposed a further refining of the breath by eliminating the pause in the breath. There is a physiological reason for this pause and it relates to how the diaphragm works (Coulter, 2001), which is explored in the section that follows.

From the perspective of Rama and colleagues, the goal is to work consciously on overcoming this pause from the beginning of one's meditation practice. They posit that if one eliminated the pause in the breath one would never die of a heart attack, a smooth continuous breath being associated with a proper functioning heart. A complete explanation of this aspect of controlling the breath has to do with making the exhalation and inhalation equal and eliminating the pause in the breath.

Why would the authors propose eliminating the pause when the adepts' breath seems to be suspended? As the student progresses, the pause becomes a source of extraordinary experience, but balancing the health of the individual comes first. A good example of the effects of working with the breath related to good health is evidenced in research conducted by the HeartMath Institute (McCraty, 2015). The findings lend support to what the ancients observed in themselves and relayed to us through the breath awareness skills cultivated to achieve success in meditation. With the relationship of the heart rate to breathing and positive emotion, HeartMath researchers suggested that autonomic nervous system imbalances are associated with (McCraty, 2015, p. 22):

- Depression
- Irritable bowel
- Hypoglycemia
- Fibromyalgia
- Panic disorder
- Hypertension

- Sleep disorder

- Asthma

- Premenstrual syndrome (PMS)

- Fatigue

- Anxiety

- Dizziness

- Migraine

As the adepts found, one can balance one's autonomic nervous system simply by being aware of the breath and making some gentle modifications to one's less than conscious habit. The point is that the beginner needs to understand good healthy breathing before seriously considering holding his or her breath—the pause—to mimic advanced meditative states.

Diaphragmatic Breathing

Continuing with the idea of working with the breath, one might wonder just how the ordinary person could consciously modify the breath. The first step is simply being mindful of breathing habits. Another aspect of consciously controlling the breath has to do with the diaphragm, a structure that any good singer or wind instrument player uses to its fullest.

The average person breathes 12 to 15 or more times per minute, and it is not uncommon for people to breathe even faster (Coulter, 2001). With that breathing rate go a related heart rate, blood pressure, muscle tonus (contraction), and ductless gland secretions. Cortisol, a hormone released during a stress reaction, is one of the ductless gland secretions. Fortunately, you can modify your breathing rate. Success with this requires an experiential understanding of the anatomy and physiology of breathing itself. Generally, the norm of 12 to 15 or more breaths per minute occurs in people whose diaphragm is locked.

Renowned physician and psychotherapist Alexander Lowen (1975) explained that a locked respiratory diaphragm is a source of a range of problems. This habit shuts us off from fully experiencing the lower half of our body and what naturally occurs there, from proper digestion to procreation. Related to the Wilhelm Reich observation regarding the breath and neurotic tendencies with which this chapter opens, some researchers have noted that a high frequency of breathing is inversely related to ego strength (Grossman, 1983). Ego strength is a factor that determines how an individual will handle unfavorable conditions.

The locked diaphragm is the source of chest (thoracic) breathing. If we observe the breathing of the average person, we see distinct chest movement up and down, sometimes even involving the shoulders. On a less than conscious level, this is keeping the nervous system in a heightened state sympathetically. It is a breathing pattern that keeps us ready for flight or fight. Recall, the emphasis is on maintaining homeostasis in the ANS. The locked diaphragm habit is contrary to what the adepts or present-day therapists who work with the breath would say is good for us (Fried & Golden, 1989).

When the diaphragm is locked, it prevents oxygenated air from reaching the deeper recesses of the lungs. The significant factor here is gas exchange, getting oxygen into the bloodstream and carbon dioxide out. As biology teaches us, oxygen needs access to available blood cells in the lungs to be properly distributed throughout our system. Due to gravity and systemic arterial pressure factors, the perfusion of blood is greater in the lower part of the lungs. A locked diaphragm prevents oxygenated air from effectively reaching this blood, hindering an efficient gas exchange, and making for a more rapid breathing pattern in an effort to get the required amount of oxygen into the system.

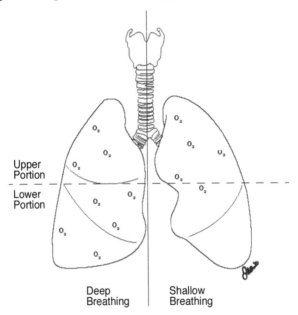

Figure 6. Lung oxygenation. © 2017, Jennifer Hollis, MS, www.hollisvisualizations.com

The right side of Figure 6 is indicative of a diaphragm that is locked and the left side is indicative of a diaphragm that is engaged. The left side indicates oxygenated air being drawn into the deeper recesses of the lungs by the action of an engaged diaphragm. When the diaphragm is locked, as indicated in the right side of the figure, the oxygenated air does not get pulled into the lung's deeper recesses, causing the gas exchange to be less efficient. Following on this is rapid, shallow breathing that is not conducive to meditation or a stress-free lifestyle.

You can easily check the functioning of your diaphragm while lying on your back. Unless there was some previous trauma to your system, you will probably find that your abdomen rises and falls as you inhale and exhale, respectively. This shows a natural relationship between the movement of the diaphragm and your abdominal muscles. Notice what happens to this relationship when you sit. What happens to the movement of your abdomen?

Check what happens by placing one hand on your chest and your other hand over your navel and observing your hand movement as you breathe. Unless you have had some training in breathing, you will probably notice that the abdomen has ceased its movement; the primary movement related to breathing has changed its location to the chest. Some people will have movement in both hands and others will have dominant motion in the abdomen. The latter is an indication of abdominal diaphragmatic breathing.

A slower balanced breath alters the heart rate, blood pressure, muscle tension, and hormone release in the body. You can check several of these without the aid of any medical devices. Considering the parameters of the relaxation response, we can see that engaging the diaphragm could be very important. It is conceivable that a breathing rate could readjust from a norm of 12 to 15 or more times a minute to four to eight times a minute just by virtue of mindfully engaging diaphragmatic breathing. The implications are that the breathing pattern for the norm has its own ANS parameters and a trained breathing pattern results in a more healthy state. We, the authors, have seen the results of understanding the breath and relaxation. We worked with hypertensive patients in the Rehabilitation Department of the charitable Himalayan Institute Hospital Trust in northern India. Under the direction of the medical director, patients who wanted to control their hypertension without medication were sent to work with us. We simply taught them to breathe and relax, nothing else, and the results were a decrease in baseline blood pressure. Training in self-regulation methods is a key factor.

Understanding that our breathing habits can affect our ANS is something extraordinary, part of the profound knowledge the adepts have related to us. Some would say this knowledge was secret, but the secret, literally speaking, was always right under our noses.

The Breath and the Chakras

The breathing process and bringing the ANS into harmony is a key element in all the meditation traditions, but the masters from the East have taken the observations to another level. The things they observed about the breath are astounding, and there are still many facts about the breath that are unknown to the average person. These masters understood the relationship between the breath and what are popularly known as the chakras, which have some correlation to the major nerve plexuses of the central nervous system.

There is a relationship between the chakras and an ancient way of viewing the elements of creation. Eastern tradition identified five elements: earth, water, fire, air, and ether. The tradition of Swara yoga holds that the direction the breath exits the nostrils indicates which element is active in the universe of the individual's body. (One might also say it indicates where along the CNS, at which nerve plexus, the less than conscious mind is located.) Each of the five chakras from the base of the trunk to the neck is related to an element. The element that interested the Eastern masters the most was the element ether, located at the neck plexus. This element was evidenced when there was no obvious direction of the breath exiting the nostrils, just a faint sense of warmth. This seeming disappearance of breath direction was a sign that the mind had moved to a subtler realm. This condition of the breath was a step toward achieving the actual meditative state.

Channel Purification

Another tool that can be used for the balance of the autonomic nervous system is channel purification. These subtle energy channels, called *nadis* in yoga science, are similar to the meridians in traditional Chinese medicine. Two of the prominent channels can be accessed via the nostrils. Channel purification involves consciously controlling the flow of breath, alternating breathing out and in through one nostril at a time until an extraordinary event takes place: the full and simultaneous opening of both nostrils.

The brain's hemispheres have a relationship with the nostrils and, accordingly, the breath. An often-overlooked fact is that the nasal cavity is an entry point into the emotional brain, the limbic system. This happens via the olfactory bulb, which is a gateway to the limbic system. The olfactory bulb is at the top of the nasal cavity. Neurophysiologists have long known the effect of odor or fragrance on the olfactory bulb, but it is also affected by air passing over it.

Many people know that the right hemisphere of the brain is associated with the left side of the body and the left hemisphere is associated with the right side of the body. The left nostril is related to the right hemisphere and the right nostril to the left, per the adepts. The adepts were clear about the importance of these relationships long before science considered questions of brain laterality.

Some of the contested theory that circulates around hemisphere dominance suggests that left-brain activity is related to analytical thinking. Right-brain activity is related to more artistic, feeling-oriented activity. The left is associated with more of a masculine quality, the right more of a feminine. These are generalizations, of course. The adepts observed, however, that hemispheric activity changed in the course of a 24-hour period, and it did so in regular intervals, every one to two hours. They also observed that they could alter their hemisphere dominance at will. They did this by understanding their breath and the relationship of their nostrils to brain hemisphere dominance.

Channel purification is a tool to help us manipulate the brain. Why is this important for the practice of meditation? The adepts understood that when air was flowing equally in both nostrils, they experienced a state they termed "happy mind." Equal nostril airflow was a sign that both hemispheres of the brain were activated equally.

Everyone has had this "happy mind" experience, but few have paid attention to its relationship with the breath or nostrils. We have all had the experience of being somewhere and, all of a sudden, for no reason associated with the events surrounding us, or maybe in conjunction with those events, we experience a quiet joy, a happy mind. The next time this phenomenon happens to you, stop and notice your nostril dominance. You may find that both nostrils are completely open. Meditation masters know that a well-trained individual can achieve this state at will. It just requires mindful practice.

The adepts say this happy mind phenomenon is a prerequisite for meditation practice. They noticed that when an individual was breathing mostly from the left nostril, that person's attention was drawn to the thoughts just below the surface of the conscious mind (Freud's "preconscious"). When an individual was breathing mostly from the right nostril, the concerns were mostly with the physical body. When breathing through both nostrils, neither of these concerns was relevant; the mind was happy, content, and the process of deepening the subtlety of the person's awareness could occur.

The relationship between nostril dominance and hemisphere dominance as well as meditation's impact on the brain is fascinating. Some researchers argue that meditation is a right hemisphere–mediated experience. The meditation master's observations are: If both nostrils were not open, then the best nostril to have open to make an approach to meditation is the left nostril, which reflects right hemisphere activity.

Many of us will struggle with all this attention paid to breath awareness and meditation practice, thinking perhaps we can circumvent what the adepts have observed. The truth is that either our intention is strong enough to take us to this hemisphere-balanced state at will, like the adepts, or we have to work with the breath, visualizations or sounds, or a combination to achieve this goal. The condition of the nostrils, brain, and breath is evident in one who has achieved the meditative state. Those who are practiced at working with the breath, understanding how it affects the mind, making it serene, and altering the activity of the brain hemispheres are well on their way to the simple awareness necessary for advancing with meditation. Remember, the breath follows the mind and the mind follows the breath.

If working with the breath alone is a challenge for a person, concentrating on a physical object, sound, or visualization will produce the same results regarding the breath, the brain, and the meditative state. The meditation masters have left us with many tools or approaches for achieving success with meditation. If we model them, we will have good results.

One of the authors (Charles) had the opportunity to verify the connection between hemisphere dominance and nostril dominance at the Meditation Research Institute on the campus of Swami Rama Sadhaka Grama in Rishikesh in northern India. He reports: I was hooked up to a 64-pin EEG and produced right hemisphere, parietal lobe activation in a range of less than three cycles per second (delta, the brain-wave activity of deep dreamless sleep) while focusing on left nostril–oriented channel purification. I produced the same on the left hemisphere side, while doing right nostril–oriented channel purification. This alteration occurred within just a few minutes.

We, the authors, once asked our master teacher, Dr. Swami Rama, a physician, scientist, and adept, for his thoughts on the tools of technology and the insights they provide. He said, "If we had had such things in our cave monastery, our novices would have advanced much quicker."

Working with the Breath

What if we took conscious control over the attributes of the breath discussed in this chapter? What if we experienced a stressful life event that threw our breathing out of harmony and we then worked ourselves back to homeostasis? The implications are that we could have a profound effect on our health if we took responsibility for how we are breathing. For example, a good suggested even breathing rate is about six breaths a minute, that is five seconds inhale and five seconds exhale, engaging the diaphragm. The authors' experience is that, even given individual instruction over a period of time, people often have trouble achieving this goal. We noted in yoga classes and in private sessions that it is about more than just forcing your breath to change.

When working with the breath, you may need to address fear associated with doing so, the self-preservation instinct: no breath, no life. Charles explains: Our mentor asked me to the front of an audience he was addressing and posed a question as he put his hand over my nose and mouth and prevented me from breathing. He asked, "What are you thinking about?" My eyes widened at being short of breath and seeing this he took his hand down. I said, "All that I thought about was breathing. I felt I was going to suffocate and die!" He said, "Precisely!" This was a demonstration for the audience and me of the instinctual nature of self-preservation related to breathing, and how, on a less than conscious level and more, we have to deal with this when working with the breath in any way. Changing the way you breathe is a worldview-changing event!

Working with the breath and relaxing are means of desensitizing emotionally charged events. Interventions such as autogenic training (guided relaxation used by psychotherapists) and systematic desensitization rely heavily on the relaxation response, but it often takes considerable time for effects to emerge. EFT can often produce similar results in a matter of minutes. Researchers have observed that EFT has a much more rapid effect on releasing emotional distress than the relaxation response (Feinstein, 2008; Feinstein, 2010).

This does not negate the importance of breath awareness, however. Modifying our less than conscious breathing habits provides continuous balance in our ANS and, in turn, in our lives. Furthermore, this can be tested in the laboratory of our own bodies, at no cost to us other than time.

As a note on relaxation, your ANS, your brain, and your breath, we leave this chapter with the words of our master teacher: "A well-trained individual should be able to access the relaxation response in a matter of seconds!"

5

Meditation, EFT, and Emotional Purification

An important aspect of meditation practice is emotional purification, that is, not identifying with, not being mentally attached to, disturbing emotions that inevitably arise in the process of sitting in silence and turning inward. The adepts would explain this as objectively observing those events, and here is where EFT is profoundly effective. EFT is for those things that bubble up from the unconscious and plague us. Conceivably, with EFT, one could cut down the processing time of dealing with these emotional upsets from a few days, weeks, months, or years to a few minutes or hours. As an intervention in such instances, EFT is a tool extraordinaire.

The way to emotional purification is through what the adepts call nonattachment or dispassion. As noted previously, the adepts say dispassion is a prerequisite for attaining the authentic meditative state. It often takes considerable time for a meditator not to be attached to the content of the mind-field: good, neutral, or bad thoughts.

The adepts address dispassion by offering an approach to developing it.

Dispassion and Disassociation

The initial effort with dispassion involves our understanding that emotional purification, if nothing else, is a goal. We understand how it can benefit us and begin to see how we are conditioned to respond or act in ways that may or may not be beneficial for us. We then discern what our strengths and weaknesses are and start to abandon what is not useful. Ultimately, we come to understand the fault of our attachments, of our poor perceptual habits, and become neutral toward them.

Jerry, Jerry, and Bharati (2007) use the term "dis-identification" or "dis-association" to explain dispassion. They distinguish the term "dis-association" from the medical term "dissociation," which is linked with pathology. A comparison can be made between EFT's effects on us after a negative emotional event has been cleared and the dispassion or dis-identification meditators are trained to cultivate.

Through dis-identification, one learns to observe thoughts objectively. Here is an example. Sit where you are comfortable. Be aware of your breath, feel the breath at your nostrils. Notice the breath's movement and how it feels entering and exiting your nostrils. After establishing a few moments of breath awareness, bring to mind three life events. Pick one event that is neutral to you emotionally, one that is pleasant, and one that is unpleasant.

Once you have come up with these three events, put them aside and return to your observation of the breath. Is your breath quiet? Is it smooth? Is the length of your inhalation and exhalation similar or different? Keep your breath in your awareness as you bring before your mind's eye the emotionally neutral situation. Note any effect on the breath. Then return to just observing the breath.

Then bring before your mind's eye the unpleasant situation and note the effect on your breath as you observe it. Once registered, return to the observation of the breath alone; let the negative thought go.

Lastly, consider the pleasant event and observe its effect on your breath.

Depending on your ability to pay attention to subtle differences in the breath, you may or may not have noticed any difference in how these three thoughts affected it. A perceptive person could notice the effect that each thought had on the breath.

How does this relate to meditation and dispassion? A goal of meditation is to learn to observe all three kinds of thoughts, all three kinds of life events, with equanimity. This is a disturbing consideration for most of us. Why would we want to experience all three events the same way? The secret is related to the true goal of meditation. Meditation is a practice that can get us beyond the mind as we know it.

Consider what researchers have termed automatization, "the building up of motor and perceptual habits" (West, 1990). De-automatization, or dis-identification or dispassion, reduces our habitual responses to stimuli.

The habitual responses may be unwanted, unwelcome, or unclear, as they occur on a less than conscious level.

Through the exercise of the three thoughts and observing the breath, you can learn how to reduce your habitual motor and perceptual habits associated with those thoughts. When all three thought events exert no effect on the breath, you have achieved the dispassion that is optimal for meditation, per the masters.

Meditation as Exposure Therapy

Meditation could be considered a form of what psychology calls "exposure therapy." The exercise of noting the effects of the three different kinds of thoughts on the breath is an exposure protocol.

Feinstein (2010) defines exposure protocol as a person being exposed to an unpleasant event over and over until the person is desensitized to the event. Wolpe (1958), the most noted proponent of exposure therapy, called it "systematic desensitization." In this therapy, a person is presented with the stuff of the unconscious, whether related to PTSD or another disturbing perceptual habit, and learns that dis-identification is the way through or around it. A new learning supersedes an earlier conditioning, resulting in the extinction of the problem. Clients of this therapy shift from a victim point of view to an observer's point of view.

The act of maintaining autonomic nervous system (ANS) balance in the face of events bubbling from the unconscious is similar to what occurs in systematic desensitization. EFT accomplishes ANS balance. In one study, however, EFT (imaginal exposure and tapping) was statistically superior to a session of imaginal exposure and diaphragmatic breathing as an intervention (Feinstein, 2008; Feinstein, 2010).

We, the authors, posit that EFT can help meditators work through the muck of their less than conscious minds, especially those troublesome recurring thoughts and feelings that hinder or even stop their progress in meditation. The goal of meditation from a psychotherapeutic perspective is more often than not stress reduction and emotional purification, and it is used as a means of readjusting a person to his or her environment. The same could be said of EFT.

Learning to view life events with equanimity is the challenge of meditation and life. Managing anger, greed, and selfishness and working with bad perceptual habits requires the dispassionate observation of these behaviors as they come before the mind's eye. When dis-identification is developed via meditation, the results manifest in day-to-day life. We become more mindful in daily life and make better choices.

The process of learning to dis-identify with our thoughts, and systematically progressing with meditation helps us avoid what John Welwood calls "premature transcendence" (Fossella, 2011). Premature transcendence is trying to rise above the raw and messy side of our humanness before we have fully faced and made peace with it. In premature transcendence, we tend to use absolute truth to disparage or dismiss relative human needs, feelings, psychological problems, relational difficulties, and developmental deficits (Fossella, 2011). The authors posit that the emotional purification through EFT practices such as the Personal Peace Procedure (clearing the emotional charge on all the disturbing events of one's past) helps prevent any such tendencies in any serious student of meditation.

The final dis-identification, the neutrality toward all things that come into the mind-field, is the aim of meditation, emotional purification being both a precursor and a product of achieving the goal. The mindfulness-based practices of meditation facilitate living in a state of perpetual harmony. EFT is an excellent tool to speed through unpleasant exposure-type events that occur during meditation. Without emotional purification, there is no possibility for accessing the self-existent reality, a balanced enlightenment. Expediting emotional purification is the promise that EFT holds for achieving long-term success with a meditation practice.

When dis-identification in meditation is mastered, there is the knowledge reminiscent of peak experience states, but on a permanent basis. Some of the aspects of this knowledge are: the dichotomies, polarities, and conflicts of life tend to be transcended or resolved; fear, anxiety, inhibition, defenses, confusion, and conflict decrease or disappear; and fear of death disappears (Maslow, 1970).

EFT Exercise:
Nostril Dominance and Developing Dispassion

EFT is an effective tool for developing dispassion toward difficult emotional events and noticing other phenomena related to meditation. As an illustration of this, the following is a script from one of the simple exercises offered in an introduction to basic EFT. In this case, the authors presented the exercise to an audience of hypnotists.

Presentation Leader (PL): I would like everyone who would like to join in to pick something that they wish had never happened. Nothing too intense, just some minor irritant that you wish had never happened. In addition to this, I would like you to take an assessment of how you feel physically. Do you have a minor ache or pain that you notice every now and again? Is it with you this morning? I would also like you to pay attention to the breath at your nostrils. See if you can discern through which nostril your breath is flowing more freely. Any questions? We will explain the significance of these things later.

Audience Member (AM) 1: What if you can't tell about the nostrils? Don't I always breathe out of both nostrils?

PL: Remember the last time you had a cold? Were both nostrils clogged up at the same time? This is a gross example, but think about it. Some of you will say yes here and some no. It is a matter of observation. If this doesn't come readily, forget about it. If you can make all three observations, good; if only one or two, good.

AM1: Okay.

PL: Now let's tap through the basic points, at least two times. Just tap, nothing else. [Everyone was guided through EFT's Basic Recipe twice.] What is your experience? What happened to the discomfort or tension you felt, if any? What is your nostril dominance at this moment compared to before, and how does that minor event you wish had never happened look and feel now?

AM1: That minor event does not seem to have any charge associated with it.

AM2: Yes, that's my experience also.

AM3: The minor discomfort I had with my shoulder seems to be gone. [AM3 rotated her shoulders, as if searching for the discomfort.] No, it's really not there.

AM4: My nostril dominance changed.

PL: Did it change from right to left or left to right?

AM4: They both seem to be open. What does that mean?

AM5: My nostril dominance changed also, but they are not both open.

PL: [to AM1] How do you feel about the change in your event? What was the initial emotion associated with it?

AM1: I don't have any feeling about it. It's as if it doesn't matter anymore. I'm no longer angry about it! It seems to me as if I had been holding a balloon and now I have just let it fly away.

PL: So the event seems to have lost its emotional charge and you can view it in equilibrium?

AM1: It seems so. [Pause] Absolutely. Wow!

Being able to view things dispassionately in a relaxed condition and the ability to affect hemisphere dominance are prerequisites for advanced stages of meditation. Until then, we practice from where we are and progress steadily. Mindfully understanding the relaxation response and working with the breath, a sound, or an image will do until our capacity jibes with our intention. This is the way of the adepts. We will touch on this more later.

6

The Supramundane Aspect of Meditation

Meditation is the lab work of spirituality.
—Swami Veda Bharati

Shapiro (1980) suggests that meditation was developed as a means to establish insight, emotional purification, and concentration as well as bring about altered states of consciousness. The process of meditation, in turn, changed an individual's perception and understanding of the nature of reality.

Meditation as an altered state may be a misnomer. The adepts suggest that the ultimate state one recognizes by means of meditation is really the normal state, and the other states that we experience such as waking, dreaming, and deep sleep are the altered states. What is really meant by "altered state"? What we usually think of as an altered state can be achieved via hallucinogens, alcohol, and similar substances. Shapiro (1980) suggests that the altered state be viewed as a continuum from profound, intense, but more common alterations of perception to full-blown mystical or spiritual experiences.

The interest a person has in meditation early on might be an indicator for what he or she will experience, or not. Those interested in self-regulation will certainly experience its benefits. Those who yearn for something deeper, the supramundane, the transcendent, may have such experiences. It may be, however, that no matter from which direction you approach meditation, you experience both results.

The Brain and the Supramundane

The reasoning behind the conclusion that everyone who practices meditation regularly will experience both the mundane and supramundane results is the very nature of the practice and its effect on the brain. When we practice meditation, we are directly affecting the brain (Davidson & Lutz, 2008). Neuroscience has confirmed this, suggesting that meditation actually increases the thickness and volume of the gray matter of the brain (Hölzel et al., 2010). The gray matter is the outer cover, if you will, and its increase in volume and thickness in certain areas of the brain is significant per neuroscientific research on meditators. Gray matter naturally shrinks with age. Currently, increasing the thickness and volume of gray matter is thought to be better for cognitive health in old age. The ancients demonstrated their awareness of the connection between meditation and the brain in their allusions to the fabled "lotus of a thousand petals" in the head.

In *Evolution's End: Claiming the Potential of Our Inheritance*, Joseph Chilton Pearce (1992) explained how our brain and its structures relate to the evolutionary process of human behavior. Pearce considered three primary areas: the reptilian brain, the mammalian brain, and the new mammalian brain. Pearce paralleled each area to a stage of human development.

The reptilian brain is the most primitive of the three and is that part of the brain structure that relates to the primary urges: physical survival, food, shelter, procreation, and territory. These are the primitive urges we humans share with all animals.

The limbic system is the emotional brain—the mammalian brain. Theorists hold that what makes the human different from the snake is emotion.

What truly sets us apart is our cortex—the new mammalian brain. The cortex gives us the ability to reason (Pearce, 1992). Recent research has shown that meditation activates the prefrontal cortex. Left side anterior activation is associated with positive emotions and reduced anxiety. Meditation also increases the thickness of the frontal cortex, an area that is important in the regulation of emotions. Meditation also enhances the areas of the brain important for moral decision-making, attention, learning, and memory (Raine, 2014).

Neuroscientist Andrew Newberg and colleagues mapped the cortex during meditation and posited an explanation for the transcendent experiences that people have (Newberg, D'aquili, & Rause, 2001). They identified four areas of the brain affected by meditation: visual associated area, orientation associated area, attention associated area, and verbal associated area.

It seems obvious that the visual associated area of the brain is stimulated if visuals, mystical or otherwise, arise in meditation practice. The orientation area orients the body in space and makes the distinction between self and other. The "self" is notably a mental representation. Interestingly, this association area also has a left and right hemisphere orientation. The left hemisphere is related to the mental sensation of a limited physically defined body, and the right is related to the sense of the spatial coordinates by which the body can be oriented.

The attention-associated area of the prefrontal cortex is thought to be related to the will. This area can have increased activity during meditation and is known through brain scans to be important in various religious and spiritual states.

The verbal area is located at the junction of the temporal, parietal, and occipital lobes and is key in creating abstract concepts and relating them to words (Newberg, D'aquili, & Rause, 2001). This last area is thought to be connected to causal thinking linked with the creation of myth and how myth is expressed in ritual. All of this effort was spent to explain a neurological basis for the mystical experience. This effort is termed "neurotheology," and Newberg has been at the vanguard of the field. The adepts would take exception to the discussion of meditation as having any theological connotations at all. They would also take exception to the physical brain being able to apprehend or register the truly transcendent experience. We will consider this next.

The Mystic Quest

As mentioned earlier, the debate between the quantum consciousness paradigm and the psychoneural identity thesis paradigm, and between mystic and dogmatic theology paradigms, has been ongoing since ancient times. Today, in all three of the monolithic religions, there are adherents who consider meditation culturally alien or contrary to their religious tradition.

To discover that meditation poses no threat to any religion, all one need do is look deeply into the body of knowledge found in the mystical literature of these traditions. All three religions have interior traditions whose practices match those of mystics the world over. One reason that these interior traditions are met with suspicion, and also a reason that science shuns them, is the subjectivity of the mystic experience. Another reason might simply be that people have trouble with the concepts mystic, mystical, and mysticism. Many people avoid the internal aspects, the deeper aspects of their tradition, based on their lack of understanding of these terms.

In the classic *Dictionary of Philosophy* by Dagobert D. Runes (1960), the entry for the word "mysticism" traces its origin to the mystery religions in which there was the mystes, the initiate, who knew the secret or saw through the veil. The idea of an initiate implies esoteric or hidden knowledge. This leads some to consider meditation to be esoteric knowledge, but the adepts say otherwise.

Before classifying meditation as esoteric, we should consider what the word "esoteric" really means. Something is esoteric, hidden, or for the few only as long as more people don't avail themselves of the knowledge. The average person can access the tool of meditation, meditation being something that can introduce you to yourself on multiple levels. Through the practice of meditation, individuals will find that they are applying the axiom of Plato and other sages: Know thyself.

Those who follow Plato's lead (Neoplatonists and others) would define mysticism as a belief in the possibility of union with the divine by means of ecstatic contemplation. Plotinus, a famous Neoplatonist, was said to have lost himself in such contemplation for hours while standing gazing at the horizon. He explained his experience as a flight of the "Alone to the Alone," the all-one to the all-one.

Evelyn Underhill, an important proponent of mysticism, expounded upon it in her classic work, *Mysticism* (1961). Mysticism is a spiritual quest to find the "way out" or the "way back" to some desirable state where one can satisfy one's craving for absolute truth. Underhill explained that the true mystic has succeeded where others failed in establishing an immediate communication between the spirit in the human and the one being called by various names by the religions, philosophers, and, now with the advent of quantum physics, scientists.

Underhill (1961) established that mysticism is not opinion, philosophy, or the pursuit of occult knowledge. It is the achievement here and now of the immortal heritage of humankind, and is the art of establishing a conscious relation with the absolute. The practices of meditation seem significant when we look at what Underhill

(1961) cites as some of the definitive markers of true mysticism:

- Mysticism is practical, not theoretical.

- Mysticism is an entirely spiritual activity, "spiritual" meaning the transformation of the lower mind so that it becomes capable of perceiving subtler and higher realms.

- The business and method of mysticism is love.

- Mysticism entails a definite psychological experience. Underhill maintained that spiritual desire is useless unless it initiates the costly movement of the whole being toward the Real, a reorganizing of the whole character to understand the conscious and the less than conscious.

- True mysticism is never self-seeking.

In these parameters, there appears to be something for everyone who approaches the subject, from scientist to theist, from psychologist to philosopher. In Underhill's explanation, we see allusions to the mundane and the supramundane. Even so, her perspective alone may not be enough to dispel the controversy surrounding mysticism. The controversy may simply reside in how religion itself is understood.

Scholars and psychologists have considered the phenomena that Underhill documented. Comparative religion scholar Ninian Smart (1995) provides some food for thought on the mystic quest relevant to religion. Smart's paradigm for religion in general comprised six components:

1. The experiential

2. Ritual
3. Myth
4. Social
5. Ethics
6. Dogma

The supramundane aspect of meditation is ultimately working toward a direct encounter with the experiential. Smart's explanation of the experiential is difficult to understand. Here we borrow the words of Rudolph Otto (1981) to try to explain the experiential as an encounter with something that is wholly other, an experience that is tremendous, awe-inspiring, mysterious, and fascinating. The experiential can also be explained as the self-existent reality, a reality beyond the mind's ability to comprehend that has existed since beginning-less time.

Connections can be made to Underhill's ideas about mysticism and the experiential. The mystic is little concerned with the external trappings of religion and is solely concerned with the experiential. This has often put the mystic at loggerheads with the established order.

Regarding the experiential, William James agreed with Underhill that it involved a definite psychological experience and transformation. He wrote that it was too awesome to speak of, there was some revelation of knowledge involved with it, the phenomenon was transient, and it could not be brought about consciously (James, 1958). The adepts would agree with James, with the exception of his last point. The adepts propose meditation as an activity to put oneself in a position to be receptive to the experiential.

Finding the Meditation Method That Suits You

The approach we take to meditation depends on our nature. We each have a preferred way of learning, a way that is most comfortable. The adepts were more than familiar with this, as a result of their intense understanding of human nature. Based on individual learning styles, a person is attracted, or directed by a preceptor, to a specific approach to meditation.

In this book, our first consideration for meditation is as a tool for self-regulation, a mindfulness tool related to breath and body conditions, a mostly kinesthetic, that is, a seemingly physical orientation. This is one approach. Other approaches might be more visual in their orientation and others more auditory.

In keeping with the concept of different learning styles, Shapiro (1980) suggested approaches for learning meditation based on three different types of learners (Table 1).

Approach to Meditation	Learning Style Verbal/Auditory	Learning Style Visual	Learning Style Tactile
External orientation (outgoing person)	Chanting of mantra or special syllables or words	Mandala/yantra or other symbols or fixed point/object	Touching thumb to each finger or using prayer beads
Internal orientation (more introverted type)	Mantra or special syllables or words (mental recitation)	Third eye Crown of the head Symbol or image	Heartbeat, Breath

Table 1. Suggested Meditation Objects and Meditation Learning styles

Meditation is considered part of a science, and the meditation masters have gone into great depth in delineating approaches to meditation. Bharati (2006) indicates that meditation is an integrated grid whose methods are interconnected in definite sequences, along definite paths related to the different "dimensions of the constituents of human personality." Examples are the 256 different forms of concentration, and their 13,000 variants given in texts such as the Malini-Vijayottara-Tantram (Bharati, 2006). Artist and poet Paul Reps lists 120 different meditation techniques in his classic *Zen Flesh, Zen Bones*, sourced from the texts of the adepts (Joo, 2007).

Theravada Buddhists have a long tradition of providing meditation techniques suitable for different temperaments. They list six different temperaments—greedy, hating, deluded, faithful, intelligent, and speculative—and give 40 different objects of meditation for these types (Buddhaghosa, 1976).

Shah (1990) lists three different phases of developing knowledge and relates them to three phases of the spiritual development of the aspirant. In phase one, the aspirant is seeking intellectual knowledge and is solely interested in the collection of facts to elucidate other intellectual concepts. In the second phase, aspirants are interested in emotional and other states that are situations in which aspirants think they have perceived something supreme but cannot avail themselves of it. The third phase is directed at real knowledge, knowledge of the self-existent reality, with the aspirant desiring direct knowledge of the supramundane, of reality beyond the boundaries of thought and sense perception.

These three phases can be correlated to the different brain structures. A student in the first learning stage would be more involved with the primitive parts of the brain concerned with flight-fight-freeze, food, or sex. The primary relationship to the experiential would be through the emotion of fear. Overcoming fear is important for the quest. Students in the second learning stage, interested in the various states, would relate more to the emotional center, the limbic system. They would be seeking intimate emotional relationships with what they considered the experiential. The final phase is for one prepared to directly experience the supramundane, the ultimate, beyond the brain's cortex.

A person of the first type might be given practices in the self-regulation aspect of meditation. Individuals of the second type might find these same practices useful but also have an orientation toward something that stimulated them visually or something that stimulated the internal auditory faculty. Mandalas, yantras (the Vedic origins of mandalas), icons, or simply the beauty of nature could be examples of visual stimulation related to a meditation object. Sound might also be a significant element for this type of person. Mantras or words from the various traditions that instill feeling are used. Benson's relaxation response protocol used a word, any word, as a means to focus the mind (Benson, 1975). The ideas are similar, but the intention of a mantra often includes an expression of feeling or emotion. A random word or number would have no such connotation.

Being at the stage of the third type of individual presumes a level of preparedness. This seeker easily discerns the nature of reality, unfettered by an imbalanced emotional life. In most cases, this person is someone who has moved through the stages of meditation to this level of preparedness. The masters mention that what we are given as beginners to help us with meditation are simply tools, which must eventually be abandoned for the sake of something higher and subtler.

The masters understood that the human mind is not able to grasp the formless, that is, the supramundane. They ultimately categorized students as only two types: the one who needs all the practices and objects we have alluded to, and the one who does not require them. The latter is rare.

It should be understood that those who learn a systematic approach to meditation, who understand that relaxation of the body and balancing the autonomic nervous system are important, can forgo much of the frustration that often accompanies learning meditation. Some people have access to technology that helps them move through this understanding faster, but remember that the ancients had only their own bodies and minds. The one thing no technology or technique can get you around is the workings, good or bad, of your mind.

Peak Experiences and Unitive Consciousness

Abraham Maslow (1970) relayed his notions about being receptive or not to what he called "peak experiences." Regarding these experiences, his clients reported the following:

- The whole universe is perceived as an integrated and unified whole.

- The experience was ego-transcending, self-forgetful, egoless, unselfish.

- The experience was like experiencing universality and eternity.

- Emotions such as awe, wonder, reverence, humility, and surrender before the greatness of the experience.

- A loss, even though it was transient: of anxiety, of inhibition, of defenses and control, of confusion, of conflict, of the fear of death.

Maslow (1970) explained unitive consciousness, a phenomenon often occurring during peak experiences, as "a sense of the sacred glimpsed in and through the particular instance of the momentary, the secular, and the worldly."

Newberg, D'aquili, and Rause (2001) present a state they call Absolute Unitary Being (AUB) to express something similar to unitive consciousness. In the AUB state, there are no discrete objects or beings, no sense of space or time. There is only an absolute sense of unity—no thought, no words, no sensation. AUB is where the mind exists without ego, in a state of undifferentiated awareness.

Mystics of all stripes speak in terms similar to the observations of Maslow and Newberg. One example is the Hesychasts, who were a group of Eastern Orthodox mystics that had habits similar to those of meditators the world over. Hesychast practices are thought to have begun with the early desert fathers of the church and still exist among monks on Mount Athos in Greece and elsewhere. The four characteristics of Hesychast practice, as given to the authors via personal communication by Catholic theologian and monk turned swami Justin O'Brien, ThD (Swami Jaidev Bharati), are: (1) a striving toward a state of total rest or quiet (this could be equated to Benson's quiet environment and decreased muscle tonus); (2) the repetition of a patterned group of words or a phrase (similar to Benson's use of a mental device); (3) practices designed to help concentrate the mind, such as physical immobility, control of the breath, and internal focus; and (4) a feeling of inner warmth and a physical perception of "divine light."

To consider another way EFT might fit in with the progression of a meditative lifestyle, we can look to Maslow's hierarchy of needs, which begins with the most basic and primitive needs and moves up from there as follows (Huitt, 2007):

1. Physiological: hunger, thirst, bodily comforts, etc.

2. Safety/security: out of danger

3. Belongingness and Love: affiliate with others, be accepted

4. Esteem: to achieve, be competent, gain approval and recognition

5. Cognitive: to know, to understand, and explore

6. Aesthetic: symmetry, order, and beauty

7. Self-actualization: to find self-fulfillment and realize one's potential

8. Self-transcendence: to connect to something beyond the ego

Early psychology was directed at harmonizing the ego to the everyday world. The so-called Third Force psychologies, Maslow being a representative, recognized a much loftier goal. Meditation's goal is still more lofty. Meditation's goal, per the adepts, is to allow us to be permanently stabilized in the self-existent reality, the condition of transcendence while functioning in the world.

Hindrances on the way toward this stabilization in Maslow's hierarchy of needs are: lack of belongingness and love, lack of self-esteem, and lack of understanding (cognitive aspect). These three areas would be the most obviously related to the emotional purification that EFT can help us with by releasing held emotional pain. This emotional pain is what prevents us from being self-actualized—being self-fulfilled and living to our potential. EFT has the ability to help us clear the blocks to all the resources we have within. Blocks removed, we can then experience the awe-inspiring self-existent reality to which the adepts allude.

With EFT, Why Do We Need Meditation?

If EFT helps us clear out small and large traumas of the past, leading to a richer, fuller, and happier life, why do we need meditation? For some, the answer would be that we don't. But for those who are drawn to go beyond, who feel the supramundane beckoning them, meditation is a tool to enrich and deepen their understanding.

Looking at our being as though composed of five sheaths, a model from an ancient Indian philosophy called Vedanta, can help explain this. This paradigm explains all levels of reality from the mundane to the supramundane. The sheaths are five aspects of our being, all of which are subject to constant change.

The following explains the five sheaths, progressing from the grossest to the subtlest:

1. **Body Sheath:** The sheath that makes up our physical body is kept alive by food and kept healthy with a good diet, exercise, and relaxation. It can be thought of as a sort of first level of command, giving us a tool to interact with the world and take in information through the senses. When this level is off balance, we experience pain and discomfort, making it hard to think clearly and get things done. We can use EFT tapping to eliminate or lessen pain and help make it easier to live in this physical "home" that we use to experience life.

2. **Energy or Breath Sheath:** This sheath is the vehicle through which the breath moves, carrying on it the vital energy to sustain life. It provides the energy to do whatever we do, from movement to thinking to emoting to communing with the Divine. We tap into this level with breath work, energy work, and mindful movement practices such as yoga, tai chi, and qigong; deep relaxation exercises; and acupuncture and acupressure. The points we are tapping on in EFT are acupuncture points (points close to the surface of the skin that are points in the body's energy channels called "meridians"). We could also say they are points in the energy sheath. By

working at the level of the energy sheath, we can affect both the mind and the body. In this paradigm, the breath sheath is shown to be the link between the body and the mind. When we affect this level, we can experience physical sensations (e.g., I feel less heaviness in my chest, my breath is deeper), energy sensations (e.g., I feel tingling in my body), mental effects (e.g., How I was thinking now seems silly to me—it makes me laugh; now I see why I was protecting myself), and emotional effects (I feel so angry at my brother for what he did to me as a kid). EFT can be used to address the sensations and effects that need to be cleared.

3. **Mental Sheath:** This is the level of the mind that interacts with the world, passes on information to subtler levels of the mind, and puts into motion decisions that are then carried out by the body. Our habit patterns, beliefs, and values are associated with this level. The personality traits that make us what we've become are located here (the Eastern philosophy called Vedanta defines personality as a series of habit patterns).

As we consider the material residing at this level, we are able to understand why we have put our energy into certain activities, people, and circumstances and not others. With tapping, we start to see our limiting beliefs, childhood enculturation (in EFT, called "writing on the walls"), and patterns we have developed to protect ourselves as well as protect those we love. Perhaps, as a child, we used food to buffer ourselves from physical, verbal, or sexual abuse, or became a "perfect kid" who never demanded anything so that our parents had an easier time. As these patterns come up from the unconscious, we are afforded the opportunity to reevaluate how well they are serving us now, and make the necessary changes to move forward in life. Again, tapping can help us here.

4. **Discrimination Sheath:** This level of our mind is responsible for decision-making, discrimination, and, when quiet, for receiving intuitive flashes. If we procrastinate on making decisions and acting on them within a reasonable time according to what life presents to us, we lose the opportunity to learn and grow—to evaluate the consequences of our decisions and learn what works and what doesn't work. Making decisions and evaluating their effects helps fine-tune our discriminating ability. Tapping can help us realize that we need to act on something, decide on something we're sitting on, or pay closer attention to what our inner voice is telling us to do. As we achieve more internal quietude, it's easier to hear what our inner voice is saying and profit from this advice.

5. **Bliss Sheath:** To experience this level, we need to go beyond tapping. It is the subtlest level of our material being and closest to our spiritual essence. For the adepts, everything that is subject to change, death, and decay is considered matter. Mind is considered matter because mind is always changing. This level of mind is extremely subtle, and we need to be very quiet physically and mentally to experience this level—quieter than we can get even with tapping. There is bliss related to bodily experience and then a bliss the adepts say is beyond. It is this "beyond" level we are referring to here. As we move inward, we can experience this subtle level in deeper

states of meditation, prayer, or contemplation. Since bliss is our spiritual essence, experiencing our spiritual self leaves us naturally blissful, regardless of what's happening in our life.

Examining the model of the sheaths gives us an additional framework for studying how the different levels of our being interact with and affect each other. For example, a person may not be aware that she gets angry when criticized by her father. She does, however, notice a pain in her throat at these times (physical sheath). The emotional pain (mental sheath) of being criticized by her father manifests in her body, as she holds back on expressing her anger.

Another person may have a hard time owning his overbearing nature. When he meditates, it comes up and disturbs him (mental sheath). He is frustrated because that has been his way of being in the world and he doesn't know how to change it. With an understanding of the five sheaths, he can opt to do breathing practice (energy sheath) to obtain a more neutral stance on this personality trait, as well as to soften his way of being.

Tapping naturally tunes us in to the first four sheaths. We can tap on (1) physical symptoms and sensations (body sheath level); (2) on the breath (breath or energy sheath), as in EFT's constricted breathing technique whereby we evaluate the depth of our breathing before and after tapping (see Chapter 2); (3) on personality traits (mental/discrimination sheaths), as when we tap on being introverted, being fearful in social situations, or being unable to follow through on the goals we set; and

(4) on decisions we have made (discrimination sheath), such as: "I've tried to please my mother all my life instead of following my own inner voice," "I wish I had gotten a higher-paying job," or "I hung out with the wrong people and got into drugs."

Beyond the five sheaths that make up our temporal being lies our true Self. It goes by different names in different spiritual and religious traditions. We can call it pure light, love, truth, spirit, pure consciousness, or God. Per the adepts, this is ultimate reality, never subject to change, death, or decay. The objects of the world do not affect it. It is our true nature, that which underlies everything else in the world. To reach it, we must be still: "Be still and know that I am God" (Psalms 46:10). As we listen with nonphysical ears, we go beyond what our mind understands.

Another way of looking at this unnamable aspect of our being (call it what you will, the self-existent reality, the quantum consciousness of the quantum physicists, pure consciousness, or any of the other names we humans have used to attempt to explain the unfathomable, the unspeakable, the unimaginable, the experiential) is presented in the ancient text Mandukya Upanishad. In that text, our human experience is divided into three states: waking (W) state, dreaming (D) state, and deep dreamless sleep (DS) state. Our lives rotate through these three states from the moment we are born until we die. Figure 7 depicts the brain-wave activity of each of these states.

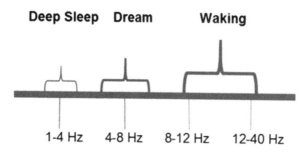

Deep Sleep   Dream   Waking

1-4 Hz   4-8 Hz   8-12 Hz   12-40 Hz

Figure 7. A simplified depiction of the brain-wave frequencies of waking, dreaming, and deep dreamless sleep states.

The W state would encompass activity in the range from 8-40 Hz, the D state from 4-8 Hz, and the DS state from 1-4 Hz. Each of these states is depicted as a tic on a much broader line, a broader line representing a substratum from which the tics emerge. We can think of EFT, psychotherapy, hypnosis, and rudimentary meditation as activities that interplay in the tics on that broader line.

The broader line is the substratum from which all else emerges. Meditation is a tool the traditional goal of which is to provide a way to experience the substratum, to rest in that substratum, to be the substratum, the core of our being.

In this chapter, we have looked at all the components of our being and levels of human development from systems such as Maslow's peak experiences, Vedanta's theory of sheaths, the Hesychast's four major practices, neuroscience's brain development, Ninian Smart's components of religious experience, and Underhill's qualities of mystical experience. Our goal is for you, the reader, to understand the complexity of your being and the stages of inward movement. These stages range from the physical to the energetic to the psychological to the spiritual, and beyond the first steps of spirituality to the experience of unitary consciousness, which is beyond words, mind, and a separate sense of self. As you understand the inward journey, you can better assess where you are on that journey, what your strengths are, what resources you can use to move further inward, and how all the levels of your being can be optimally used to achieve your goals.

Your goal in meditation might be stress reduction, developing deeper focus and concentration, or experiencing what the mystics have experienced. Whatever your goal, it is helpful to have a wide array of tools to choose from in reaching it and a good theoretical foundation from which you can map your journey.

7

How to Use EFT to Enhance Your Meditation

If meditation or other spiritual practice leads us to experience the subtlest and most rewarding parts of ourselves, why should we tap? Why not just practice meditation? If the systematic practice of meditation helps us deal with our fears, problems, and habit patterns, why do we need tapping? This chapter explains why tapping is so helpful not only for enriching our daily lives, but for aiding progress in meditation as well.

According to Jerry, Jerry, and Bharati (2007), there are many ways that Energy Psychology can assist a meditation practice, including:

1. The logistics of meditation: achieving a still and comfortable posture

2. Overcoming resistance and obstacles to meditation

3. Letting go of fear

4. Letting go of attitudes and mental states that are not helpful to meditation such as boredom, impa-

tience, not feeling like meditating, neglecting to make time to meditate, and regarding meditation as not working

5. Addressing challenges that arise in meditation

6. Dealing with challenges that arise in following ethical guidelines

7. Letting go of perceived stresses

8. Bringing the energy body back into balance

9. Overcoming psychological reversal

10. Overcoming or managing restless states of mind

Let's explore each of these in detail and see how EFT can help.

Easing the Physical Logistics of Meditation

In order to progress in meditation, we need to sit with the head, neck, and trunk straight, and be in a still, steady, and comfortable position. This is a preliminary to accomplishing depth in meditation and lays the groundwork for progress. Sitting still is not as easy as it seems, as anyone who has tried it knows. What arises when we try are distractions such as: my back hurts, my foot's asleep, I lose awareness and start to lean to the side, I get fidgety and can't sit still, and many more. EFT tapping on these challenges can help clear them, along with our reactions to them, so the physical body can be positioned straighter and be more comfortable. When EFT facilitates a relaxed body, meditation happens more easily.

Overcoming Resistance and Obstacles to Meditation

Whatever reasons and excuses people come up with for not meditating, there is an EFT Setup Statement available to get past it. The mind gets creative in finding excuses. A few of them are: I'm too extroverted to meditate, nothing ever happens when I try it, I don't have the time, I get up too late and have to get ready for work, I start off well and soon after get out of the routine, my hip hurts when I sit on the floor, and I can't quiet my mind. Many of these have simple solutions such as: Sit on a chair, go to bed earlier, and/or practice breathing before you meditate. However, underlying these reasons are unconscious blocks of which we may be unaware. These often involve the sense that, during meditation, something will come up from the past that has to be looked at and dealt with and that is affecting not only our meditation practice, but also many other areas of our lives. All the more reason to clear it out! Tapping is an excellent tool and helps here.

Tapping setups that can be used to overcome resistances include the following. There are many more — as many as there are different minds!

Even though I'm too busy to meditate, I love and accept myself anyway.

Even though by nature I'm outwardly directed, I love and accept myself anyway.

Even though it's hard for me to maintain a regular meditation routine, I love and accept myself anyway.

Even though my body hurts when I sit on the floor, I love and accept myself anyway.

Even though my mind runs wild when I meditate, I love and accept myself anyway.

Letting Go of Fear

Various fears arise during meditation: fear of the unknown, fear of losing body awareness, fear of getting estranged from your spouse or partner who isn't interested in meditation, fear of seeming weird to your friends, fear that your outlook on life will change, fear that you won't succeed (so why bother). The adepts would say that all fears fall into one of three categories: fear of experiencing pain, fear of not knowing enough or being wrong, and fear of ceasing to exist. You can tap away all of the fears that arise during meditation. Often, a deeper fear emerges that can also be tapped on, leaving you with confidence that it is possible to experience subtler states of being.

Tapping can be used to quell fears. Some examples of Setup Statements for fear include:

Even though my friends will think something is wrong with me, I love and accept myself anyway.

Even though I fear losing my sense of self if I meditate, I love and accept myself anyway.

Even though I won't know who I am or where I am if I lose body awareness, I love and accept myself anyway.

Even though my partner and I might lose our connection if I meditate, I love and accept myself anyway.

Even though I fear investing time in meditation and failing to experience anything, I love and accept myself anyway.

Releasing Unwanted Attitudes

Releasing unwanted attitudes such as boredom, impatience, not wanting to meditate, not taking time to meditate, and regarding meditation as not working overlaps somewhat with resistance and obstacles but includes some variations on the theme. Practicing meditation day in and day out is a challenge, especially when we feel that nothing is happening. Because we often aren't tuned in to subtle shifts that take place when we meditate, it's easy to think we are wasting our time. The outcome of this is to decide that there's no point in bothering, because there is no return on our effort.

Long-term meditators know that something is always happening in meditation. If you practice regularly, even for just a few minutes a day, you can look back to how you were six months ago, a year ago, five years ago, and 10 years ago and definitely see change.

Not perceiving these small daily changes can lead to a sense of boredom and loss of enthusiasm for practicing. There are as many Setup Statements in this area as there are unwanted attitudes. A few include:

Even though I just don't want to meditate because it's so boring, I love and accept myself anyway.

Even though I'm not a patient person, I love and accept myself anyway.

Even though I have more important things to do, I love and accept myself anyway.

Even though I don't feel anything at all is happening when I meditate, I love and accept myself anyway.

Even though I think meditation works for other people but not for me, I love and accept myself anyway.

Even though I got into this thinking it would be different, I love and accept myself anyway.

Even though I feel like I'm not accomplishing anything when I meditate, I love and accept myself anyway.

How many of the feelings and behaviors expressed in these Setups apply to you? What others come up for you? Tap on those as well. You can also change the love and acceptance part of the Setup to: "I choose to sit every day anyway." That will help emphasize that you are going to do it, no matter what excuses your mind comes up with.

A long-term meditator, Dr. David Jacobs, in his seminar "Science Meets Spirituality" in July 2010 at the Inner Peace Yoga Center in Indianapolis, Indiana, said something that resonated deeply with a lot of the seminar participants. He was discussing the challenges of maintaining a daily meditation practice. His trick for doing this was something he discovered when, at the age of 16, he took a vow to meditate every day for 20 years. His one guideline was that he would sit for a minimum of three minutes a day. His reasoning was that the effects are cumulative and anyone can practice for such a short period of time. This guideline cuts through all kinds of resistance, especially the themes of: I don't have time, it's too hard for me, and I have trouble sustaining a practice. In case you're wondering, Dr. Jacobs did succeed in meditating every day for 20 years. He almost forgot one day, but his unconscious mind wouldn't let him fall asleep that night. When it was almost midnight, he sat up in bed to meditate and then fell asleep right afterward. The power of a good habit can help us sustain our meditation practice for a long time, despite the many obstacles and resistances that may arise.

Another way to look at our ingrained attitudes is through the four functions of the mind, per the Eastern psychological perspective of Vedanta, one of the classical Indian philosophical systems. These four functions include: sensory-motor mind, ego, the decision-making/discrimination function, and the function that is the storehouse of life experiences. These four functions are constantly interacting with each other. One predominates at any given time, however.

Sensory-motor mind interacts with the world through the senses—collecting, organizing, and interpreting sensory data. It then passes on information to other functions of the mind, a decision is made about what to do, and we act based on the decision. It is here that patterns of habit, beliefs, and values are active. Much mental chatter goes on at this level.

Ego is the function of the mind that defines who we are and gives us our sense of "I-ness." It helps establish boundaries between others and us and gives us a personality from which to operate. In this regard, it is a useful function. However, it also limits us and can cause us to feel separated from others. In terms of meditation, it can create blocks for us by coming to conclusions such as: "I'm not a good meditator so why bother?" or "I want to be a good provider so I need my time for work" or "It won't help me to meditate." When we tap on limiting beliefs and blocks such as these, we open things up so the decision-making and discriminating function can come to the fore.

The function of decision-making and discrimination gives us the ability to process information and decide on the best plan of action. It is subtler and quieter than sensory-motor mind. As we fine-tune our power of discrimination, it's easier to see what to do and what to avoid doing—to see cause-effect relationships. We can see things more objectively, break out of our habit patterns, and make decisions with a more open mind and greater clarity of thought. This helps life go more smoothly and provides us with a better quality of life. We tap into our visionary capacities at this level.

The storehouse of life experiences is the part of the mind that stores everything we ever experienced. It is synonymous with the unconscious or less than conscious mind. With us not being aware of what's in there, it's easy for the stored memories to creep back into our conscious mind and affect how we feel, think, and act. More often than not, we are unaware this is happening, so we can't control it. It may show in ways such as having a mood change for no apparent external reason, having a strong reaction to someone we just met, having little confidence to succeed in a particular endeavor, or even having more confidence than is presently warranted. If we're aware of this function, we can tap on what we're experiencing, even though it may seem illogical or difficult to understand.

Addressing Challenges That Arise

Adepts pointed out some major obstacles that prevent us from going deeper in meditation and reaping its full benefits. One obstacle is sickness. As long as the body is uncomfortable and imbalanced, it is hard to sit still, breathe evenly, and concentrate. Hatha yoga (the practice of poses or asanas), tai chi, and qigong were developed to keep the body flexible and fit and help keep the internal organs healthy. EFT can be used to reduce pain and stiffness, and help us overcome habits that weaken our health, such as poor diet, excessive alcohol use, getting too little sleep, and exercising too little or too much. It may help reduce bodily discomfort from being in an accident or having had a serious illness. Here are some Setup Statements to tap on:

Even though I'm too tired to meditate, I love and accept myself anyway.

Even though I don't feel well enough to meditate, I love and accept myself anyway.

Even though I don't know how to focus my mind, I love and accept myself anyway.

Even though I'm too stiff to sit and meditate comfortably, I love and accept myself anyway.

Even though not exercising leaves me too foggy to meditate, I love and accept myself anyway.

Even though I can't meditate well because alcohol use gets in the way, I love and accept myself anyway.

Even though it's hard to meditate in the morning because of my late-night eating, I love and accept myself anyway.

A second obstacle to going deep in meditation is mental inertia, or mental laziness. When the mind is too dull to focus, it resists doing the work. Though constant practice will help the meditator overcome this obstacle in time, it is initially easy for us to say we're not in the mood to practice, to be governed by these moods, and to start to skip days of practice. These days can easily become weeks or months, until the resolve to meditate disappears entirely. Try tapping on Setups like the following:

> *Even though it's hard for me to focus, I love and accept myself anyway.*

> *Even though I'm not in the mood to meditate, I love and accept myself anyway.*

> *Even though I don't sit for meditation every day, I love and accept myself anyway.*

> *Even though doing consistent practice is a real challenge, I love and accept myself anyway.*

> *Even though I'm too lazy to practice every day, I love and accept myself anyway.*

A third obstacle is doubt. To succeed in meditation, enthusiasm and energy are needed. When doubts creep in, it's hard to be enthusiastic and exert the appropriate energy. We can tap on our doubts about succeeding or on our doubts that something deep and life changing can happen through the practice of meditation. We might also doubt that our teacher can really help us. In this case, we can tap on our resistance to following instructions given to us by a teacher or on resistance to being in the presence of people who can help us. EFT Setups like these can help:

Even though I truly doubt I can ever achieve what my teacher has achieved, I love and accept myself anyway.

Even though I'm resistant to going deeper, I love and accept myself anyway.

Even though nothing special happens when I meditate, I love and accept myself anyway.

Even though other people experience way more than I do, I love and accept myself anyway.

Even though no one can help me progress, I love and accept myself anyway.

Even though I don't like to be around people who have accomplished more than I have, I love and accept myself anyway.

A fourth obstacle is lack of enthusiasm. This can come from doubts or other sources, such as a negative comment made by a person who doesn't understand what meditation is. It can also stem from misconceptions about the process of spiritual evolution. One prominent myth is that, in a meditation practice, we go into a state of bliss and keep going back to that same place whenever we meditate. In fact, the process has its continuing ups and downs, its rich spells and dry spells, times when we feel calm and happy and times when we experience great turmoil. Tapping is a great way to dispel these limiting beliefs. Here are some sample Setup Statements:

Even though I feel sad when I meditate, I deeply and completely accept myself.

Even though I'm discouraged because meditation isn't what I thought it would be, I deeply and completely accept myself.

Even though I was enthused at the beginning but don't feel enthused now, I deeply and completely accept myself.

Even though I have to drag myself to my meditation seat, I deeply and completely accept myself.

Even though I don't feel happy that I'm doing a good thing for myself, I deeply and completely accept myself.

A fifth obstacle is sloth, or laziness. This manifests when we just don't feel like practicing and can't overcome the resistance. Maybe the mind is dull or maybe the body is dull, but the energy to overcome the resistance just isn't there. Diet can be one of the causes here; being sure to eat a moderate diet rather than overeating can help rekindle energy and enthusiasm. EFT can be a great help with these obstacles, with Setup Statements such as:

Even though I just don't feel like meditating, I deeply and completely accept myself.

Even though I think meditation is just too hard and I don't feel like doing it, I deeply and completely accept myself.

Even though my mind is dull, I deeply and completely accept myself.

A sixth obstacle is craving for the pleasure of the senses. We're on task and then get distracted by the things around us. Desires can draw us to sensory objects including food, drink, sleep, sex, shopping, smoking, gambling, and video games, to name a few. Any desire that dissipates our energy and leads our focus away from our goal would fall in this category. You can dispel your cravings by tapping on Setup Statements such as:

Even though I'd rather sleep in than meditate, I love and accept myself anyway.

Even though I waste valuable time and energy on the Internet, I love and accept myself anyway.

Even though I eat too much heavy food and then have trouble meditating, I love and accept myself anyway.

Even though the Internet keeps me from going to sleep on time, I love and accept myself anyway.

Even though drinking alcohol makes it harder for me to meditate, I love and accept myself anyway.

A seventh obstacle is false perception, or wrong views. Our faulty decision-making ability keeps us from understanding what to give up and what to pursue. It keeps us from understanding the stages of spiritual progress. If we're in a dark mood, we conclude that we're not doing well. In fact, this temporary darkness can be a sign of great progress. It can be a sign that something heavy inside of us is releasing. If we persevere, we eventually get out of the darkness, feeling lighter, brighter, and freer. Tapping can help here:

Even though I am in a dark mood, I deeply and completely accept myself.

Even though I get discouraged because I don't feel like I'm accomplishing anything, I love and accept myself anyway.

Even though I feel worse now than before I was meditating, I love and accept myself anyway.

An eighth obstacle is the inability to attain higher ground. We want to progress, but just don't seem to get anywhere. It is frustrating and can lead us to quit. Because progress in meditation is subtle, we don't see the small steps of progress that we are making each day. It seems like we're getting nowhere when in fact we are moving toward higher ground and making more progress than we realize. Try tapping on Setup Statements such as these:

Even though I get frustrated by my lack of progress, I love and accept myself anyway.

Even though I feel like I'm spinning my wheels with meditation, I love and accept myself anyway.

Even though I feel like giving up, I love and accept myself anyway.

Even though I'd rather quit than struggle with meditation, I love and accept myself anyway.

Even though I don't see any progress at all, I love and accept myself anyway.

Sometimes in meditation, we have an experience that is totally pleasant, different from what we have ever experienced. We assume that will be the norm from then on, and are surprised and disappointed when it isn't.

This is a ninth obstacle: the inability to maintain a higher level of consciousness once we have initially achieved it. Tapping can be used even on subtle experiences like this:

>*Even though I experienced such quietude in meditation, and am so frustrated that I can't get back to that place, I deeply and completely accept myself.*

>*Even though I want to go back to the depth I experienced earlier but don't know how to get there, I deeply and completely accept myself.*

Dealing with Ethical Challenges

In the West, we have the Golden Rule. A similar Eastern code is the Ten Commitments. They are guidelines to follow to feel clear and peaceful within and have a harmonious relationship with others. The Ten Commitments include five activities suggested to refrain from and five things to actively do. The five Restraints are: non-harming, non-lying, non-stealing, not overindulging the senses, and non-possessiveness. The five Observances are: purity, contentment, austerity, self-study, and surrender to a Higher Power.

One or more of these challenge most of us. Being content is a common challenge. We always want to be in a different place than we are. It is hard for us to be content in our present situation. This is not to say that you shouldn't strive to be better or have goals you want to attain. It simply means accepting your starting point and working from there. Any frustration, disappointment, embarrassment, or other emotion that arises from being where you are can be tapped on.

The following is an example of tapping language for someone who wants to be a dynamic public speaker but has trouble speaking even in front of a small group.

Setup: *Even though I want to be speaking in front of large groups but am afraid, I deeply and completely accept myself. Even though my heart beats so fast when I get up in front of people, I deeply and completely accept myself. Even though it's hard to imagine being relaxed in front of people, I deeply and completely accept myself.*

Reminder Phrases:

Everyone will be looking at me.

I'm scared.

What if they think I'm stupid?

What if I stumble over my words?

My heart beats so fast when I'm in front of people.

My hands get sweaty.

I'm so self-conscious when people look at me.

What will they think?

Releasing Stress

Stress affects our health on all levels, and when our health is compromised our meditation practice is less effective. EFT is able to clear the emotional charge we have on a disturbing event because it halts the body's stress response. Research has shown that EFT actually reduces the level of the stress hormone cortisol (Church, Yount, & Brooks, 2012). Any life challenge we are dealing with can be tapped on to release stress.

One of the best EFT methods to use to clear all the issues that contribute to our stress level is the Personal Peace Procedure (see Chapter 2). Write a long list of everything that is bothering you and has ever bothered you. What has made you angry? Jealous? Sad? Frustrated? Discouraged? Greedy? Think of all the people you feel resentment or other negative feeling toward. Also think of the things you need to forgive yourself for. The list should be quite long if you write down anything and everything that comes to your mind. The good news is that once you tap on some of the memories and issues, others will release or lessen in intensity on their own, without tapping specifically on them.

If you keep tapping on a regular basis, the list will not have a chance to grow large again. Then tapping, along with breathing and relaxation, will help you go into meditation with a more settled body and clarity of mind. You will be less reactive during the day, triggered by fewer things. All of this will aid your meditation practice. Here are some Setup Statements to tap on to reduce your stress reaction to events or circumstances in your everyday life:

Even though I'm so annoyed with my coworker, I love and accept myself anyway.

Even though I had a bang-up fight with my spouse, I love and accept myself anyway.

Even though I'm angry with myself for messing up my presentation, I love and accept myself anyway.

Even though I ate all those doughnuts when I promised myself I wouldn't, I love and accept myself anyway.

Even though I'm scared to go to the party, I love and accept myself anyway.

Even though my head is pounding with this approaching deadline, I love and accept myself anyway.

Even though I'm anxious about passing the test, I love and accept myself anyway.

Rebalancing the Energy Body

A strong and balanced energy system aids meditation practice. Without this, we are more likely to get sick, have trouble sitting still, have a harder time regulating our breath, and find it harder to focus and quiet the mind. Tapping balances the flow of energy in the body. Even if we tap without saying anything, there will be a regulating effect. Any time we tap on an issue, we are further straightening out our energy system, making it a little easier to meditate.

Although we can't see this energy, the ancients have known about it for millennia. Using this concept, the Chinese observed the meridian system and developed acupuncture, and the Indians observed the system of nadis and incorporated it into esoteric yoga. If you have ever had an acupuncture treatment or have done yoga, you may have experienced some inner shift firsthand. If not, you can experience it easily using EFT. When you tap and start to feel more relaxed, breathe more easily, and let go of a formerly troublesome challenge, then you know from the evidence that your energy has shifted. You are no longer in the state of stress from emotional disturbance, physical pain, or whatever your tapping focus was. Here are some examples of such tapping:

Even though I still feel troubled about the exam, I am more relaxed since I started tapping.

Even though I still have a headache, it is less intense since I started tapping.

Even though I was tense at the thought of talking to my boyfriend, I now feel more relaxed and at ease.

Even though my breath is still restricted, it is much deeper than it was before I tapped.

Overcoming Psychological Reversal

As discussed in Chapter 2, Psychological Reversal refers to the concept that when our energies are blocked or reversed, we develop symptoms. It is often compared to "putting batteries in backward." It could also be viewed as neurological disorganization. It often happens outside our awareness and is caused by negative thinking. When it is present and uncorrected, it blocks us from making progress and achieving our goals. Psychological Reversal is at work when a professional athlete goes into a slump or when someone has a chronic disease that doesn't respond well to conventional treatment. Another example is when someone tries to lose weight and can't; they are consciously saying they want to, but are unconsciously saying, "Why bother, I'll only gain it back" or "More will be expected of me if I lose weight." (The latter is an example of secondary gain, a term psychologists use to describe the benefits of maintaining a behavior or habit, as discussed in Chapter 2.)

Doing the EFT Setup by tapping on the side of the hand point or rubbing the sore spot is a quick way to rebalance the energy system and correct Psychological Reversal. Since the energy system affects both the body and mind, it stands to reason that rebalancing our energy system will have beneficial effects on our meditation practice. Here are examples of tapping language to address psychological reversal:

Even though I'll miss the attention I get by being sick, I now choose to get well.

Even though people will notice me if I'm thin, I still choose to attain a slim body.

Even though doing public speaking will take me out of my comfort zone, I want to grow more than I want to stay stuck.

Managing Mental Restlessness

By nature, the mind is always thinking. The quieter we get, the more active the mind seems to get. In actuality, the mind is busy, busy all the time. We only notice it when we take time to slow down and pay attention. Some of this restlessness stems from unresolved issues from the past. As we tap them away, we have a more calm and quiet mind and sitting for meditation becomes easier. We can ease into a meditative state in less time and stay there longer. Try tapping on Setup Statements such as:

Even though memories of my narcissistic mother keep bubbling up when I meditate, I choose to keep letting them go.

Even though that bad car accident keeps coming up when I sit, I love and accept myself anyway.

Even though it takes me a long time to calm this restless mind, I love and accept myself anyway.

With all the excuses our mind can come up with for not meditating, it's amazing any of us manage to practice regularly! The mind is very creative when it comes to getting out of doing what's helpful for us, so we need to be even more creative in training the mind. One of the major ways to train ourselves explained in this chapter is the use of EFT. It will knock down the challenges, frustrations, stresses, and discomfort we inevitably face in the process of self-purification. If you've ever tried to overcome resistance or an obstacle, then you already know you need all the help you can get!

8

A Method
of Meditation

Setting the Stage for Meditation

Meditation is a spiritual science that can be practiced by anyone. Returning to our definition of meditation—"a conscious attempt to focus attention in a nonanalytical way, and an attempt not to dwell on discursive, ruminating thought"—we can see that whatever helps us concentrate will aid our meditation practice.

What helps enhance concentration? There are a variety of physical, psychological, and spiritual factors.

Physical: Being able to sit with the head, neck, and trunk straight in a still, steady, and comfortable position aids good meditation. Sit on either the floor or a chair, but make sure you are comfortable so your mind does not focus on your physical discomfort. The goal is to be able to forget the body for some time and focus on the mind. Whatever aids in getting the body comfortable will help. This includes: a balanced diet, movement (both stretching and aerobics are helpful), sound sleep, breathing and relaxation, using the right meditation props (e.g., a firm cushion, good chair, or seiza bench, which is a low, slanted wooden bench you can sit on with your lower legs tucked under the seat), using a meditation shawl, doing bodywork, and being in a well-ventilated room with a comfortable temperature.

Psychological: Having peace of mind is essential to going deeper in meditation. Anything unresolved from the past that is disturbing our present needs to be addressed if we want peace of mind. Ultimately, anything unresolved from the past can get worked out in meditation, but it takes a lot of time. By using EFT, we can cut that time and release any angst we are experiencing related to: lack of success in meeting worldly goals, problematic relationships, lack of self-confidence and self-esteem, lack of a stable home base, addiction issues (such as food, alcohol, drugs, smoking, spending too much money, and excess Internet use), low self-esteem, lack of self-confidence, not allowing ourselves to have any fun in life, feeling like we don't have choices, not performing at peak levels, not knowing our purpose in life, lack of enthusiasm for life, and more.

Spiritual: Some people have the belief that meditation is for others but not for them because they are too extroverted, not spiritual, too busy, or have been unsuccessful in previous attempts (which were often not systematic or sustained). Anyone can practice meditation, with the exception of those with mental limitations such as schizophrenia. The drive to meditate and sustain meditation has to come from within. No one can give you the inspiration to keep going. Inspiration comes from the need to find something more in life than what the senses and external relationships can provide. It comes from a longing to experience other dimensions of reality. The deeper the longing, the easier it is to keep meditating, even when it appears that nothing is happening.

Creating a Time and Place

Meditation gets easier when you practice at the same time every day. This helps speed up progress and overcome the tendency to procrastinate or feel lazy. Unconsciously, the mind starts to gear up for that assigned time. When that time comes, your mind has already prepared itself, making it easier to sit. Like anything else you do at regular times, the body and mind start to go on automatic. A habit begins to form. If you left the house in the morning without washing up and brushing your teeth, you'd feel uncomfortable the rest of the day. If you are used to exercising at a certain time of the day and miss a day or two, your body will feel the difference. The same thing happens with meditation. If you get in the habit of sitting at a certain time of day and then skip a day, you will miss it.

Pick a time that works best for you. Choose a time when you feel alert and unrushed and that is not just after you've eaten. After eating, the body's energy is needed for digestion and it's therefore harder to concentrate and stay alert. Many people choose a time in the morning before they leave the house. This allows them to know their meditation is done and won't be circumvented by what may come up during the day. If your household is busy with the morning routine of getting ready for work or school, it's ideal to sit for meditation before all this begins.

Some people find it easier to sit at night, such as before dinner or before going to bed. This is helpful for people who are still alert at night and feel less rushed and preoccupied when the concerns of the day and their responsibilities are behind them.

For some, it is not possible to sit at the same time every day. This applies to people with indefinite work schedules (such as people who travel a lot) and people with young children, among others. In this case, simply resolve each day when you will meditate the next day.

Creating a place for meditation is relatively simple. All you need is a clean, uncluttered, and quiet space. It can just be a corner of a room. Ideally, you want a space with good air circulation, away from televisions, phones, and other distractions. Avoid sitting on a bed, as there is an association with sleep and it might be harder to stay alert. You can sit on a chair or on the floor, whichever is more comfortable and allows you to sit straight and let go of body awareness. Once your practice is established, you will find that it's easier to sit anywhere—in someone else's house, in a hotel room, in an airplane, as a passenger in a car, or at work with your office door closed.

Some people like to meditate near pictures or objects that are meaningful to them. Others like to light a candle. These are simply ways to help set the mood but are not essential to the practice itself. The main objective is to have a place where energy starts to build from your meditation occurring there regularly. It's like visiting a holy site but in your own home.

How Long Should I Meditate?

The length of your meditation depends on how long you are able to meditate and how long you want to meditate. Stay within your comfortable capacity and be guided by your level of motivation as well. Sitting for a longer time does not necessarily equate with making more progress. Practicing daily is more important than the length of time you sit. Therefore setting a realistic goal is important. It is more helpful to sit for five to ten minutes a day than to sit once a week for 45 minutes. If you sit every day, your time spent sitting will increase on its own. If you set a goal to sit too long and you are physically and/or mentally uncomfortable, you will end up fighting yourself. It's better to make the time spent as pleasant as possible, so you have a good association and want to continue.

If you have trouble being still, have doubts about the benefits of meditation or your ability to practice, or otherwise aren't motivated to sit for a long time, then sitting for a few minutes will be easier than setting a longer time goal. If, on the other hand, you are a disciplined person and have been wanting to learn how to meditate, you may find it easier to start with longer sessions, and you may even be able to practice twice a day fairly easily. Either way, as you achieve greater physical and mental stillness by paying attention to your diet, breathing, and the kinds of mental influences you take in, you will find that your mental chatter and distractibility are reduced.

Developing a Systematic Practice

To support our meditation goals, we need a workable system of practice, one that is not physically demanding, does not require us to adopt foreign habits or customs, and with which we can see change and progress.

Being systematic is important. Without it, people start and stop meditation and feel discouraged and/or distracted. At their meditation workshops, the authors often hear from participants that they used to meditate but stopped. Many learned from books without having a systematic practice or understanding of what they were trying to accomplish. Others felt that they were too extroverted or their mind was too busy for them to succeed.

In reality, all of our minds are busy, busy, busy, chattering away all day long. We only start to notice it when we sit down to quiet the mind. Plus it can be hard to notice the subtle shifts taking place in the mind, as compared to the more obvious shifts that occur in the body and breath with meditation; it often seems like nothing is happening.

Having a systematic method gives you a better chance to stick with it, notice some change and benefits, and feel confident enough to continue with a daily practice. If you pay attention, you may notice that when your body is still and comfortable, your attention naturally goes to the breath, and when your breath is well regulated, your attention naturally goes to your mind. Therefore it stands to reason that a good system would help you relax your body, then regulate your breath, then turn to watching your mind.

Many spiritual traditions begin with bodywork. Yoga has the practice of asana, or postures that coordinate with the breath to relax and strengthen the body, regulate the flow of the breath, and allow one to experience the mind-body connection. There are other body-oriented systems that do the same.

Signs of Progress in Meditation

As meditation progresses, what we are looking for is a deepening sense of quiet and stillness. The mind becomes peaceful and joyful. Some signs of progress, as explained in *Superconscious Meditation* (Arya, 1978, pp. 112–113) include:

- There are less scattered thoughts, daydreams, and distracting visuals.

- Interfering thoughts remain for a shorter period of time and are less intense.

- The mind stays focused, free of distracting thoughts, for increasingly longer periods of time.

- Stronger feelings of peace and serenity are experienced both during meditation and after practicing meditation.

- After finishing meditation, it becomes easier to remain aware of the breath and the mantra or prayer that was used to focus and stay centered while in meditation. This remembrance stays fixed more easily during daily activities.

- As time goes on, there is an increasing pull to meditate again while involved in daily life.

- Through the meditation process, one receives inner guidance on how to sustain more harmonious relationships.

- One experiences fewer emotional ups and downs.

- There is a stronger emphasis on just remaining tranquil while meditating. Expectation of "experiences" starts to drop away. It is no longer important to see and hear things; the need for an "inner show" is no longer important.

Steps for a Successful Systematic Practice

1. **Relax the body.** This can be aided by tapping through the points a few times. As indicated earlier, the authors have observed physical relaxation is a by-product of tapping. Research has validated this. Simple stretches and relaxation exercises (see the appendix for basic relaxation exercise information) help prepare the body a bit more for meditation. The adepts consider yoga postures as an aid to meditation practice, to be used as a means to an end. Stretching and limbering the back and legs can significantly increase your comfort level in meditation. Even a few minutes can be very helpful. Because yoga poses work on the body and mind, doing a few poses will gently energize you, relax the muscles, help you let go of mental stress, and increase your ability to focus.

It is beneficial after stretching to do a short relaxation of 10 minutes or less. This helps you relax even more, and helps the body absorb the full benefit of the poses. Many relaxation exercises are done lying on the back, but the mind must remain alert. There is skill involved in relaxing the body but staying mentally alert and not falling asleep. It takes practice. It's best to do shorter relaxations and remain focused than to do longer ones and drift off to sleep.

2. **Sit with the head, neck, and trunk in a straight line.** This helps you breathe better, have more mental clarity and alertness, and experience quietude more easily.

3. **Regulate the flow of the breath.** As you have learned, breathing is a powerful variable. It reduces tension in the body and increases calmness and clarity of mind. If you spend a few minutes on regulating the breath before you meditate, you will find it easier to go deeper into meditation. Taking time to breathe yields more in your meditation practice. If you are resistant to taking the time, or if strong emotions come up when you practice breathing, be sure to tap on it!

Effective breathing involves learning to:

- Breathe diaphragmatically
- Breathe evenly, with inhalations and exhalations the same length
- Breathe smoothly, with no jerks
- Breathe continuously, with no pauses
- Breathe quietly, with no sounds
- Breathe through the nose rather than the mouth

4. **Continue with breath awareness and add an object of concentration on which to focus your mind.** It can be a sound, such as a prayer that you resonate with from your religious or spiritual tradition, or a mantra. Or you can stay with breath awareness as the focal point. There are different methods of meditation in different traditions, but ultimately all of them have the goal of knowing one's essential nature. The different approaches can be compared to different paths that all lead to the summit of the mountain. Choosing one path and sticking with it is what's most important. Whatever practice you use, do it daily and with full presence.

Focusing on the flow of the breath is a simple option. You can count your breaths from 1 to 10 and 10 to 1. To do so, inhale mentally counting 1, exhale mentally counting 2, inhale mentally counting 3, exhale mentally counting 4, inhale mentally counting 5, exhale mentally counting 6, and so on up to 10. Then inhale mentally counting 10, exhale mentally counting 9, inhale mentally counting 8, and so on back to 1. Continue to count the breaths from 1 to 10 and 10 to 1. This focuses the mind and aids concentration. To slow the mind, we need to give it something to focus on. Counting your breaths helps stop the mind from engaging in its regular activities such as worrying, thinking, planning, and analyzing. If you find it hard to concentrate on counting from 1 to 10 and 10 to 1, simply adjust and count from 1 to 5 and 5 to 1.

5. **Practice witnessing.** Your mind will wander even though you give it something to focus on. The mind resists being controlled, and you might become frustrated

and irritated if you try to stop it and it won't stop. It is better to allow the mind to relax and be still, without any particular goals in mind. A good student can study and achieve all A's on tests, but meditation cannot be measured with such guidelines or methods.

Our job is to study what is coming up. Rather than making the mind empty, strive to quiet and focus the mind to deepen concentration. Study what types of thoughts and emotions are surfacing. What images and sensations are you experiencing? What memories are bubbling up to the surface? Witnessing is the process of observing what comes up without judging it. It takes practice to do this.

Strive to watch your internal states like a good scientist who is watching what happens in an experiment without judging it or trying to sway the results in a certain direction. Gradually, you will acquire the ability to inspect your own thinking process without becoming disturbed by it. When you can watch and not be disturbed by passing images, feelings, thoughts, and memories, then you will remain undisturbed by the workings of the mind. This, again, is dispassion.

6. **Use discernment** to promote or strengthen the arising thoughts that are positive and helpful to your growth. Choose to not pay much attention to the negative, weakening thoughts.

7. **Cultivate detachment.** Stop judging what is happening as good or bad. View it simply as what is presently coming up. Dispassion is watching all objectively. This helps you, eventually, not be disturbed in any situation.

8. **When you are ready to end your meditation practice, come back slowly.** While maintaining awareness of the breath and the sound (if you are using a sound), bring your focus back to your body. You can then slowly open your eyes to the floor and raise your gaze upward when you are ready, or you can place the palms of your cupped hands over your eyes (without pressing on the eyeballs), open your eyes to the palms of your hands, and then slowly lower your hands when ready.

Here is another meditation approach.

1. Relax as in the previous method.

2. Sit with the head, neck, and trunk erect.

3. Observe the qualities of the breath, counting the breaths as in the previous method or not. Consider inhaling for 5 seconds and exhaling for 5 seconds, if it is within your capacity. If there is any physical or mental discomfort doing this modification of the breath, then stop the modification and just keep making the basic observations about the breath.

4. If you are so inclined, imagine the brilliance of the sun reflecting off the surface of a large body of water, or just imagine the brilliance of the sun's light inside your head. Let that light fill your entire head. Rest in that radiance.

5. Then take your awareness to the area of the heart, and imagine a cave there. Enter the cave and notice the same brilliance of light that you have cultivated in your head. Let your entire

chest cavity be pervaded with the brilliance of that light. Rest in that radiance.

6. Let the brilliance of the light in the heart and the light in the head merge. Find a place, in the continuum between heart and head, to rest in the brilliance of the light you have cultivated.

7. (a) Bring into that resting place of light a word or sound that means love or peace or joy to you. Use one of those words, if you so desire. Rest with that sound or word in the light. (b) If the word or sound option does not appeal to you, just rest in the light.

8. Practice witnessing. Your mind will wander no matter which option you have chosen: the breath or the visualization and/or sound.

9. Cultivate detachment. Don't be attached to the thoughts that come up; just rest in the light, or the light and the word/sound, or bring your awareness back to the breath.

8. When you are ready to end your meditation practice, come back slowly. With awareness of the breath, maintain awareness of the word/sound, if chosen, and bring your focus back to your body. You can then slowly open your eyes in one of the ways suggested in the first method.

Note: Audios of these practices can be accessed digitally (see the appendix for information on where to obtain them).

9

Other Aids
to Meditation

Yoga

Yoga poses (*asanas*) are a great aid to meditation practice. In fact, the yogis developed them with that in mind. Seeing that people had more difficulty meditating when their health wasn't good and their bodies were not strong enough, they came up with a series of movements to make the body strong and balanced, internally as well as externally.

Yoga has many benefits, including: strengthening and balancing the internal organs and body systems, improving circulation, strengthening the spine, enhancing immunity, improving physical strength and flexibility, releasing excess muscle tension, strengthening the nervous system, creating emotional balance, enhancing the ability to focus and concentrate, and tuning into the part of the body where the trauma of a past event has been stored and then releasing it. When we're not sure what's bothering us, we can start to gain access through body awareness.

A prerequisite for attaining depth in meditation is being able to drop body awareness for a period of time. To do this, the body has first to be comfortable. Otherwise, one's attention keeps going back to the discomfort. Doing poses can help release physical discomfort and restless energy while building strength. Sitting in meditation then becomes easier.

EFT tapping can be incorporated with poses. The authors have experimented with blending tapping and poses with more experienced yoga students. Many of the students had been practicing yoga for five years or more, so focusing on the mechanics of the pose was no longer necessary. This freed them to observe subtler things.

One experiment began by evaluating the body before class or after doing a few warm-ups. Students found an area of concern or limitation, for example, tight hamstrings, shoulder discomfort, or lower-back weakness. They gave the issue a SUD level, did a Setup Statement three times at the side of the hand point, and tapped around the basic tapping points two times. For example, someone might tap on: "Even though I have this tightness in the right side of my neck, I love and accept myself anyway."

After that, they did more poses. Students then checked whether the issue was better after tapping and reevaluated the SUD level. If there was a change in the SUD level (there often was), they adjusted the Setup Statement as needed and tapped around the basic points once again. As a follow-up to the previous example, they might then tap on: "Even though I have some remaining tightness in the right side of my neck, it is now much looser." Then they did more poses and reevaluated the SUD level. This was done three or four times during the class.

Most students noticed a drop in SUD level, greater comfort in the area they had addressed in tapping, and greater ease or more flexibility in doing the poses that had formerly been limiting.

The limitation with this method was that we had to keep stopping and tapping. So we developed another method. This method began in the same way: finding a problem area, evaluating the SUD level, and tapping on the problem area. Then students did the postures and mentally tapped the round of points twice while in the poses. This gave them a lot more tapping time and potentially greater opportunity to lower the SUD levels. As a variation, the students mentally tapped on any points they intuited were the points they needed to tap on for that particular challenge. After going through several poses with either mental tapping method, the students reevaluated their SUD level, reworded the Setup statement as needed, and continued tapping mentally.

Which method worked the best? It seemed that all of them were helpful, but each student had a technique that seemed to work best for him or her. No rigorous study was done to evaluate the results scientifically, but using anecdotal means, most students noticed greater ease doing the poses with all methods. Some noticed a huge shift in flexibility very quickly with the method that involved the least tapping. Some found tapping physically on all the points was easier than mentally tapping through the points. For others, the reverse was true.

We also experimented with breathing. The students identified something they wanted to work on, such as: my breath is shallow, there are subtle jerks in my breath, my breath is uneven (inhalation and exhalation are different lengths), or there is a slight wheezing sound as I inhale. They assigned the issue a SUD level, did the Setup tapping, and then tapped the round of points twice. Then we did some breath work, reevaluated the SUD level, adjusted the Setup Statement, and tapped the round of points twice. This procedure was the same as the first asana procedure, only we focused on breath instead of movement; no poses were done. Again, most students noticed an improvement in the aspect of breathing that they were studying.

Essential Oils

Essential oils are another great aid to meditation practice. These oils are the aromatic, volatile liquids found in plants that are usually extracted through steam distillation. They are found in shrubs, flowers, trees, roots, bushes, and seeds. Plants not only help maintain the ecological balance of the planet, they help maintain our ecological balance as well. Plants have been used by humans throughout history and are intimately connected to our physical, emotional, energetic, and spiritual well-being.

Essential oils and plant extracts work at a cellular level, purifying and mending cells and helping to restore cells to optimal functioning (Stewart, 2010). Their fragrances also help balance mood, lift spirits, dispel negative emotions, and clear the mind.

Ancient writings indicate that aromatics were used for religious rituals, for the treatment of illness, and for other physical and spiritual needs. The Egyptians were among the first to use them, for embalming as well as for the previously listed purposes. Aromatics were used in the Middle East (the Bible contains over 200 references to aromatics, incense, and ointments), India, and China and by Native Americans. The Bible refers to numerous plants that were regularly used, including frankincense, myrrh, cedarwood, cinnamon, hyssop, myrtle, spikenard, and cypress.

Once fire was discovered, dried herbs were added to the fire and the smells traveled upward in the smoke along with the prayers of those making the offerings. There is much evidence of essential oils and herbs being used in the form of incense. Incense burners dating to ancient times have been found in Egypt and the Indus Valley of India. Depictions of people using incense have been found in ancient Egyptian carvings. The scents were used for sacred purposes and for healing. They were used in religious ceremonies, for meditation, for worship, to purify an area, and to help change a mood to facilitate religious and spiritual practices.

The Egyptians were known to have imported some of the scents they used. They were fond of frankincense and myrrh as well as cinnamon, cassia, galbanum, lotus, and rose. The Chinese favored cassia, cinnamon, and sandalwood. Native Americans favored local plants such as sage and cedar, using them in smudge sticks. Gifts of frankincense and myrrh to baby Jesus reflect the value of these oils in the Middle East.

Essential oils contain hundreds of chemical constituents, such as phenols, terpenes, ethers, aldehydes, ketones, esters, and coumarins. Each constituent aids in producing certain effects. Some are calming, some boost the immune system, some reduce physical discomfort and inflammation, some are antiseptic and antibacterial, and some facilitate better respiration, digestion, sleep, confidence, clarity of mind, or higher energy levels.

The fragrance of an essential oil can directly affect everything from emotional state to mental focus to the functioning of each organ in the body. When you inhale an essential oil, the odor molecules travel up the nose and get trapped by the olfactory membranes. When stimulated by odor molecules, this lining of nerve cells triggers electrical impulses to the olfactory bulb in the brain. The olfactory bulb then transmits the impulses to the amygdala, where emotional memories are stored, and to other parts of the limbic system as well. Because the limbic system is directly connected to the parts of the brain that control heart rate, blood pressure, breathing, memory, stress levels, and hormone balance, the oils can have profound physiological and psychological effects.

The sense of smell is the only one of the five senses that is directly linked to the limbic system of the brain, the emotional control center. Emotions such as anxiety, fear, anger, and joy all emanate from this region. A certain scent can evoke memories and emotions before we are even consciously aware of it. We react first and think later.

In a study conducted at New York Medical University, Dr. Joseph Ledoux (1989) found that the amygdala plays a major role in storing and releasing emotional trauma. If that's the case, it stands to reason that stimulating the amygdala with essential oils would further support the work done with EFT tapping and also support removing "static" from our emotional body, resulting in a quicker path to an effective meditation practice and the advent of a peaceful and purposeful life.

Will an essential oil be the answer to slipping into a deep state of meditation and staying there as long as we want? Not necessarily. The results are less direct than that. When used regularly, essential oils help us achieve and enjoy better physical health and mental health. When this foundation is laid, it is easier to meditate.

As mentioned, practitioners of prayer and meditation have traditionally used a scent such as frankincense. The scent was used as an anchor, meaning that the smell quieted the mind, and every time the practitioners smelled that scent in the future, it brought them back more easily to that quiet state, reminding them of where they had been.

Here are a few popular scents that people have used through the ages to help with meditation.

Frankincense: Used in religious ceremonies for thousands of years. Good to diffuse during meditation for grounding and purpose. Increases feelings of spirituality and inner strength. Is good for mental acuity, lifts mood, inspires balanced emotions.

Jasmine: Known for its beautiful fragrance. Helps induce feelings of calmness, is uplifting, counteracts feelings of hopelessness and indifference. Lessens listlessness, improves concentration.

Lavender: Has a sweet, floral aroma that is soothing and refreshing. Promotes feelings of calmness and comfort, supports nervous system functioning, and aids relaxation.

Patchouli: Soothing and releasing. Calming and relaxing physically and mentally.

Rose: Relaxing, calming, elevates the mind and thereby creates a sense of well-being.

Sandalwood: Calming, grounding. May help remove negative programming from the cells. Encourages deep relaxation.

Ylang ylang: Calming, enhances spiritual attunement, combats low self-esteem, filters out negative energy, boosts feelings of confidence and peace.

Diet

While having a good diet won't get you to enlightenment, a poor diet can hinder you in meditation. When people are serious about improving their meditation practice, they often become more interested in improving their diet. Foods that aid digestion, breathing, clarity of mind, a good energy level, uplifted spirits, and interest in persevering with chosen goals are foods that aid an effective meditation practice. Foods that are fresh (local and organic whenever possible), home-cooked, simple, and easy to digest are the ones that should be emphasized. These include fresh fruits and vegetables, whole grains, beans, nuts and seeds, and other lean, high-quality protein foods.

Heavy, greasy, stale foods leave us sluggish and dull. When we eat them, it is easier to fall asleep during meditation. Foods to avoid include heavy meats, fried foods, excess fat, food that has been cooked and left in the refrigerator for several days, overcooked or undercooked food, foods that don't agree with your system, and food taken when you are angry, sad, or otherwise not in a good state of mind. It is also desirable to avoid poor food combinations, as they create digestive problems and leave the mind foggy (Ballentine, 2007). Poor food combinations result when we eat a combination of foods that require different types of enzymes to digest. The body strains to provide two different types of environments, when it is designed to handle only one. An example would be eating melon after a high-protein meal. When eaten alone, melon digests quickly and only remains in the stomach for a short period of time. Protein takes longer to digest and stays in the stomach longer. Therefore when they are eaten together, the melon is trapped in the stomach for too long and starts to ferment.

We also want to avoid or limit foods that overstimulate us, making the mind racy when we sit to meditate. This includes excess caffeine, hot spicy foods, and sugar.

Initially these foods stimulate us, but afterward we are more liable to experience a letdown and a crash in our energy level.

Best of all, as explained previously, are the foods that give us a sustained energy level and leave us feeling calm, centered, and nurtured.

Sometimes it's not easy to put theory into practice. We may find ourselves saying, "I know exactly what foods are good for me, but I don't want to eat them! I'd rather load up on carbs. I love my sugar, fried food, chips, and pizza." If you study how you feel after eating such foods, you will see that some of them dull your mind, making you sleepy or less focused, and others make your mind restless and unable to concentrate. Working with your diet is a long-term project rather than a quick fix, but as you work with it, you will learn a lot about yourself, and this process of self-discovery will aid your meditation practice.

These observations can become a fun experiment in self-transformation. The key is to spend time studying what you notice and looking for cause-effect relationships. Here are some mindfulness-based practices surrounding food. Ask yourself the following questions: When do I crave certain foods? What are my triggers? What does this food remind me of? How do I feel before and after I eat it? What tastes do I like? What textures? Do I eat when I'm not hungry? When? Where? What do I eat then? What foods are comforting to me? Energizing? Which leave me feeling protected? How do holidays and family or social gatherings affect my eating?

Do I eat because the clock says it's time? Do I eat while watching TV, driving, checking email, working, or reading? What resistances come up if I decide to focus just on eating and not do anything else during that time?

The more you study and understand the less your focus is on food itself and the more it is on the underlying dynamic of your eating. As you observe, you start to see family and childhood patterns, how you use food for ways other than to nourish yourself physically, memories and beliefs you have about food and eating, your body image, and how you use food when anxious or bored, to procrastinate, to feel safe, as a social connector, as a reward, and more. Working with diet then becomes an aid to meditation, because self-awareness always benefits meditation.

On the other end of the spectrum, it is also hard to focus when you are too hungry. If you have neglected to eat and try to meditate when you are hungry, your mind will be on food and how uncomfortable you are. Perhaps your blood sugar will be out of balance. Therefore having a well-regulated diet with definite times to eat is a tremendous aid to good practice.

Being in a good state of mind when you eat is also important and an aid to good digestion. One beneficial guideline is to eat only when you are in a balanced state of mind. If you eat when angry, worried, or rushed or when you have just had an argument with someone, your body will not properly process even the best food, and toxins will form.

For best digestion, it is also important to chew food well. This is a real challenge for the average Westerner, who is typically moving from one activity to the next, always a step behind, and not wanting to waste any time. Spending time eating is often seen as a waste of time, so food is gobbled down on the run. As a result, many people never reach a level of satiety and grab for food many times a day when they're not even hungry. This is a factor in the rising level of obesity and increasing frequency of heart disease, diabetes, and cancer in America.

A good guideline to follow is to chew each bite of food 32 times—one bite for each tooth. The goal is to chew food until liquefied, as the liver has no teeth. This practice aids digestion and also clarity of mind. The mind is foggier with poor digestion. However, this guideline is sometimes taken too literally. Some people report that they only get to 24 times or 28 times in chewing and they feel they have failed. If the food is totally liquefied, then fewer times of chewing are fine. If the food is not liquefied at 32 chews, then more chewing is needed. The point is to keep the goal in mind and use 32 times as a guideline.

Chewing thoroughly is a practice in itself. By chewing more, you can learn a lot about how your mind works and see how resistant you are to slowing down and paying attention. You will also notice the true taste of the food when you take time to chew. Fast food and processed food that was once very appealing will not be so inviting when you are chewing well and paying attention. Notice how eating slowly and attentively affects other things you do that are not related to food.

Watching the effects of food on the body and mind is a good practice in mindfulness. Paying attention in daily life helps us be more skillful at paying attention during meditation time. Consider experimenting with refraining from any other activity when you are eating. When you eat, pay attention to: how well you chew your food, what foods leave you calm or agitated, how foods are affecting your body and breathing, what your hunger level is when you eat, when you feel full and have had enough, and more. The goal is to feel comfortable and sated (but not overly full) and maintain alertness and clarity of mind.

For most people, eating enough cooked food is essential to achieving this ideal state. Eating fast foods, too many cold foods, snack foods, and packaged foods is not likely to leave you in a calm, pleasant state. Overcooking food is also undesirable, as the life force has been cooked right out of it. Being vegetarian is not essential to a good meditation practice, but eating foods that keep your body and mind in balance is essential. The long-forgotten art of cooking is a great boon to your meditation practice. It's best to make slow changes, one at a time. In fact, with a regular meditation practice, your diet will most likely change on its own. Small changes over time are more desirable than abrupt changes that disturb your body and mind and which are hard to maintain.

Spacing meals away from meditation and sleep is also important. It's best to wait four hours after a full meal before you meditate (or about three hours for a lighter meal). This allows your food to digest so your mind is clear and you don't get sleepy. This is another reason why morning meditation is easier. If you sit before you eat, you don't need to deal with spacing meals away from your meditation practice. Plus, if you ate dinner relatively early the night before, you will feel light and refreshed in the morning. It is also helpful to eat your main meal at midday and have something light at night, taking the burden off your digestive system. The bulk of digestion should occur before you go to sleep, as your metabolism slows down when you sleep and food does not get digested like it does when you're awake and active.

Beverages also have an effect on the ability to concentrate. You may notice that if you drink a lot of caffeinated beverages, you experience physical and mental agitation. Sugary drinks affect blood sugar levels, with a sharp upward spike in blood sugar and then a quick crash. When the crash happens, people turn to the next sugary drink (or other form of sugar) to keep up their energy. It would be better to switch gradually to water. If you boil water in the morning and take it with you in a thermos, you can sip it during the day. This is good for detoxifying the body. You can pour it and drink it warm, which, for many people, has a soothing effect. If you prefer, you can let the water cool to room temperature.

It is best to avoid ice water. Ice water chills the body too much and makes it harder to digest food properly, leading to less efficient absorption. If you are a person who loves ice water, you can create a cooling effect in your water by adding mint or cilantro instead of ice. Therapeutic grade essential oils can also be added to drinking water. Mint oil is cooling; citrus oils such as lemon or tangerine are refreshing and uplifting.

Exercise

As we all know, moving the body is a wonderful and necessary tool for good health. As noted previously, it also supports a meditation practice. Even though we know exercise is good for us, a lot of us don't do it. The modern lifestyle makes it challenging to carve out time for exercise. Work, children, home responsibilities, and running here and there in whatever other pursuits we have take up all our time. Cooking and exercise get pushed to the bottom of our list of priorities.

Even exercising for 20 to 30 minutes, three to five days a week, would be very helpful. And modern research is showing that it doesn't have to be done all at once. Exercising for 10 minutes three times a day works, too (Perlmutter, 2013). This is a way to incorporate exercise into a packed schedule. How about 10 minutes of stretching before work, 10 minutes of walking on your lunch break, and 10 minutes more of walking or on an exercise bike or treadmill after work? There are many ways to fit in a little movement here and there. Other ideas include lifting weights, jumping rope, riding a bike, jogging, using exercise bands, or putting on music and dancing.

The important thing is to do what works for you, what is comfortable for your body, and what is something you like to do so you're more motivated to do it. In Ayurveda, the ancient Indian system of health, there are 3 B's for good health. They are: keep the body moving, keep the breath moving, and keep the bowels moving. Move your body to keep your circulation going, keep your mind clear, help the body detoxify, and release stress. Keep breathing all the time, as holding the breath is injurious to the heart. Keep the bowels moving to release from the body wastes that will leave you sluggish and foggy if not removed. The best scenario is to move the bowels as many times a day as you eat meals.

Sleep

Sleep, like food, is a physical process that can have a great effect on your meditation practice. If you sleep too little, you will probably notice that you feel drowsy when you meditate. You may have trouble staying awake. If you sleep too much, you may feel sluggish and groggy and have trouble concentrating.

Most people notice that, with a regular practice of meditation, their need for sleep decreases over time. We need dreaming at night to work out what is still unresolved in our unconscious. As we work out these challenges in meditation, we need less time to do so when asleep. We then have more waking time to do creative, productive, enjoyable activities.

Afterword

Meditation helps us explore our inner realms, those parts of ourselves that are nonphysical but whose existence we intuit. This level goes beyond language and the mind. The experiences of mystics, religious and spiritual leaders, saints, and sages reflect these realms. We are equipped to have similar experiences. Many of us have already had experiences that have opened the door into these realms, and we would like to know how to get back there at will. Meditation is a way to do that.

EFT has been shown to be effective in helping to alter our physiology in ways that help us prepare for meditation, and to be effective in helping us work through the things from our unconscious that meditation allows to surface. EFT has been shown to affect the brain in ways that can make us more inclined to do internal work like meditation, if that is our choice. We, the authors, agree with those who call EFT one of the psychotechnologies that is beneficial in aiding our emotional purification on the way to experiencing what some reckon to be beyond the mind and the energy body.

If we are serious about meditation, our lives will change. Our lifestyles will reflect our commitment to meditation. Slowly over time, as we evolve, life begins to revolve around our meditation time. We become healthier because we become more aware; meditation is a tool to help us increase the subtlety of our awareness. Using EFT, diet, essential oils, exercise, rest and relaxation, and other tools greatly aids the process. Because EFT can be done anywhere, anytime and because we often see such quick changes using it, it becomes a wonderful meditation support.

Anyone who has struggled with sustaining a meditation practice will appreciate having aids that make practicing easier. The methods discussed in this book can help you avoid spending energy in resistance and instead free up your energy to go deeper into meditation. EFT is a natural tool for creating this sense of ease.

We hope you will take advantage of the information presented in this book and do many experiments with yourself verifying the benefits of meditation and EFT.

Enjoy the journey!

References

Ajaya, S. (Ed.). (1977). *Meditational therapy*. Glenview IL: Himalayan Institute.

Arya, U. (1978). *Superconscious meditation*. Honesdale, PA: Himalayan Institute Press.

Baker, A. (1990). *They call it hypnosis*. New York, NY: Prometheus.

Ballentine, R. (2007). *Diet and nutrition*. Honesdale, PA: Himalayan Institute Press.

Benson, H. (1975). *The relaxation response*. New York, NY: Morrow.

Benson, H. (1984). *Beyond the relaxation response*. New York, NY: Times Books.

Bharati, S. V. (2006). *Yogi in the lab*. Rishikesh, India: SRSG Publications.

Buddhaghosa, B. (1976). *The path of purification*. Boulder, CO: Shambhala.

Cade, C., & Coxhead, N. (1989). *The awakened mind: Biofeedback and the development of higher states of awareness*. Longmead, UK: Element Books.

Carrington, P. (1990). *Managing meditation in clinical practice.* In M. A. West (Ed.), *The psychology of meditation* (pp. 150–172). New York, NY: Oxford University Press.

Church, D. (2013). *The EFT manual* (3rd ed.). Santa Rosa, CA: Energy Psychology Press.

Church, D. (2015). *EFT for PTSD* (3rd ed.). Santa Rosa, CA: Energy Psychology Press.

Church, D., Yount, G., & Brooks, A. J. (2012). The effect of Emotional Freedom Techniques (EFT) on stress biochemistry: A randomized controlled trial. *Journal of Nervous and Mental Disease, 200,* 891–896.

Coulter, D. (2001). *Anatomy of hatha yoga.* Honesdale, PA: Body and Breath.

Davidson, R. J., Kabat-Zinn, J., Schumacher, J., Rosenkranz, M., Muller, D., Santorelli, S. F....Sheridan, J. F. (2003). Alterations in brain and immune function produced by mindfulness meditation. *Psychosomatic Medicine, 65*(4), 564–570.

Davidson, R. J., & Lutz, A. (2008). Buddha's brain: Neuroplasticity and meditation. *IEEE Signal Processing Magazine, 25*(1), 176–174.

Delui, M. H., Yari, M., Khouyinezhad, G., Amini, M., & Bayazi, M. H. (2013). Comparison of cardiac rehabilitation programs combined with relaxation and meditation techniques on reduction of depression and anxiety of cardiovascular patients. *Open Cardiovascular Medicine Journal, 7,* 99–103.

Elman, D. (1964). *Hypnotherapy.* Glendale, CA: Westwood.

Fehmi, L. G., & Robbins, J. (2007). *The Open-Focus brain: Harnessing the power of attention to heal mind and body.* Boston, MA: Trumpeter Books.

Feinstein, D. (2008). Energy psychology: A review of the preliminary evidence. *Psychotherapy: Theory, Research, Practice, Training, 45*(2), 199–213.

Feinstein, D. (2009). Controversies in energy psychology. *Energy Psychology: Theory, Research, Treatment, 1*(1), 45–56.

Feinstein, D. (2010). Rapid treatment of PTSD: Why psychological exposure with acupoint tapping may be effective. *Psychotherapy: Theory, Research, Practice, Training, 47*(3), 385–402.

Feinstein, D., Eden, D., & Craig, G. (2005). *The promise of energy psychology: Revolutionary tools for dramatic personal change.* New York, NY: Jeremy P. Tarcher/Penguin.

Fossella, T. (2011). *Human nature, Buddha nature: On spiritual bypassing, relationship, and the dharma—An interview with John Welwood.* Retrieved February 19, 2017, from http://www.johnwelwood.com/articles/TRIC_interview_uncut.pdf

Fredrickson, B. L., Cohn, M. A., Coffey, K. A., Pek, J., & Finkel, S. M. (2008). Open hearts build lives: Positive emotions, induced through loving-kindness meditation, build consequential personal resources. *Journal of Personality and Social Psychology, 95*(5), 1045–1062.

Fried, R., & Golden, W. L. (1989). The role of psychophysiological hyperventilation assessment in cognitive behavior therapy. *Journal of Cognitive Psychotherapy, 3*(1), 5–14.

Goleman, D. (1995). *Emotional Intelligence.* New York, NY: Bantam.

Goswami, A. (2008). *God is not dead.* Charlottesville, VA: Hampton Roads.

Green, E., & Green, A. (1977). *Beyond biofeedback.* New York, NY: Delacorte Press/S. Lawrence.

Groesbeck, G., Bach, D., Stapleton, P., Banton, S., Blickheuser, K., & Church, D. (2016). *The interrelated physiological and psychological effects of EcoMeditation: A pilot study*. Presented at Omega Institute, Rhinebeck, New York, October 15, 2016.

Grossman, P. (1983). Respiration, stress and cardiovascular function. *Psychophysiology, 20*(3), 284–300.

Hall, P. (1999). The effect of meditation on the academic performance of African American College Students. *Journal of Black Studies, 29*(3), 408–415.

Hölzel, B., Carmody, J., Vangel, M., Congleton, C., Yerramsetti, S., Gard, T., & Laza, S. (2011). Mindfulness practice leads to increases in regional brain gray matter density. *Psychiatry Research, 191*(1), 36–43.

Hoss, R., & Hoss, L. (2010). The Dream to Freedom technique, a methodology for integrating the complementary therapies of energy psychology and dreamwork. *Energy Psychology: Theory, Research, and Treatment, 2*(1), 45–58.

Huitt, W. (2007). Maslow's hierarchy of needs. *Educational Psychology Interactive*. Valdosta, GA: Valdosta State University. Retrieved from http://www.edpsycinteractive. org/topics/conation/maslow.html

James, W. (1958). *The varieties of religious experience*. New York, NY: Mentor Books.

Jerry, M., Jerry, M., & Bharati, S. V. (2007). *Chariot of Sadhana*. Bloomington, IN: Unlimited.

Joo, S. L. (2007). *Vijnana Bhairava: The practice of centering awareness*. Varanasi, India: Indica Books.

Kaufman, M. (2005, January 3). Meditation gives brain a charge, study finds. *Washington Post*. Retrieved from http://www.washingtonpost.com/wp-dyn/articles/A43006-2005Jan2.html

LeDoux, J. E. (1989, September). Rationalizing thoughtless emotions. *Insight*.

Leskowitz, E. (Ed.). (2014). *Sports, energy, and consciousness.* North Charleston, SC: CreateSpace.

Liou, S. (2010). Meditation and HD. HOPES (Huntington's Outreach Project for Education, at Stanford), Stanford University, CA. Retrieved from http://web.stanford.edu/group/hopes/cgi-bin/hopes_test/meditation-and-hd

Lowen, A. (1975). *Bioenergetics.* New York, NY: Coward, McCann & Geoghegan.

Mascaro, J. (1973). *The dhammapada.* New York, NY: Penguin.

Maslow, A. (1970). *Religions, values, and peak-experiences.* New York, NY: Penguin.

McCraty, R. (2015). *Science of the heart: Exploring the role of the heart in human performance* (Vol. 2). Boulder Creek, CA: HeartMath Institute.

Newberg, A., D'aquili, E., & Rause, V. (2001). *Why god won't go away.* New York, NY: Ballantine.

Newberg, A. B., Wintering, N., Khalsa, D. S., Roggenkamp, H., & Waldman, M. R. (2010). Meditation effects on cognitive function and cerebral blood flow in subjects with memory loss: A preliminary study. *Journal of Alzheimer's Disease, 20*(2), 517–526.

Otto, R. (1981). *The idea of the holy.* New York, NY: Oxford University Press.

Palmer, G., Sherrard, P., & Ware, K. (1995). *The Philokalia* (Vol. 4). London, UK: Faber & Faber.

Parker, S., Bharati, S. V., & Fernandez, M. (2013). Defining yoga-nidra: Traditional accounts, physiological research, and future directions. *International Journal of Yoga Therapy, 23*(1), 11–16.

Pearce, J. C. (1992). *Evolution's end: Claiming the potential of our inheritance*. San Francisco, CA: HarperSanFrancisco

Perlmutter, D. (2013). *Grain brain*. New York, NY: Little, Brown.

Raine, A. (2014). *The anatomy of violence*. New York, NY: Vintage.

Rama, S., Ballentine, R., & Ajaya, S. (1976). *Yoga and psychotherapy: The evolution of consciousness*. Honesdale PA: Himalayan Institute Press.

Rama, S., Ballentine, R., & Hymes, A. (1979). *Science of breath: A practical guide*. Honesdale, PA: Himalayan Institute.

Rothbaum, B. O., & Foa, E. B. (2007). Cognitive-behavioral therapy for posttraumatic stress disorder. In B. A. van der Kolk, A. C. McFarlane, & L. Weisaeth (Eds.), *Traumatic stress: The effects of overwhelming experience on mind, body, and society* (pp. 491–509). New York: Guilford.

Runes, D. D. (1960). *Dictionary of philosophy*. New York, NY: Philosophical Library.

Sapolsky, R. (1994). *Why zebras don't get ulcers*. New York, NY: Henry Holt.

Saraswati, S. M. (1984). *Swara yoga: The trantric science of brain breathing*. Munger, India: Bihar School of Yoga.

Selye, H. (1978). *The stress of life*. New York, NY: McGraw-Hill.

Shah, I. (1990). *The way of the Sufi*. New York, NY: Arkana.

Shapiro, D. (1980). *Meditation: Self-regulation strategy and altered states of consciousness*. New York, NY: Aldine.

Shapiro, D. A. (1990). Implications of psychotherapy research for the study of meditation. In M. A. West (Ed.), *The psychology of meditation* (pp. 173–188). New York, NY: Oxford University Press.

Smart, N. (1995). *Worldviews: Crosscultural explorations of human beliefs*. Englewood Cliffs, NJ: Prentice-Hall.

Speca, M., Carlson, L. E., Goodey, E., & Angen, M. (2000). A randomized, wait-list controlled clinical trial: The effect of a mindfulness meditation-based stress reduction program on mood and symptoms of stress in cancer outpatients. *Psychosomatic Medicine, 62*(5), 613–622.

Stewart, D. (2010). *The chemistry of essential oils*. Marble Hill, MO: Care Publications.

Thie, J., & Thie, M. (2005). *Touch for health*. Camarillo, CA: Devorss.

Underhill, E. (1961). *Mysticism*. New York, NY: Dutton.

West, M. A. (Ed.). (1990). *The psychology of meditation*. New York, NY: Oxford University Press.

Wolpe, J. (1958). *Psychotherapy by reciprocal inhibition*. Palo Alto, CA: Stanford University Press.

Appendix: Resources

Suggested Reading

Adams, A., & Davidson, K. (2011). *EFT comprehensive training resource level 1*. Santa Rosa, CA: Energy Psychology Press.

Adams, A., & Davidson, K. (2011). *EFT comprehensive training resource level 2*. Santa Rosa, CA: Energy Psychology Press.

Ballentine, R. (Ed.). (1986). *The theory and practice of meditation*. Honesdale PA: Himalayan Publishers.

Church, D. (2013). *The EFT manual* (3rd ed.). Santa Rosa, CA: Energy Psychology Press.

Crenshaw, C. (2014). *Pathless path: god, grace, guru: An African-American life transformed through yoga and meditation*. Rishikesh, India: Ahymsa.

Goleman, D. (1988). *The meditative mind: The varieties of meditative experience*. New York: G. P. Putnam.

Kaplan, A. (1982). *Meditation and kabbalah*. York Beach, ME: Samuel Weiser.

Life Science. (2014). *Essential oils desk reference* (6th ed.). Lehi, UT: Life Science.

Nuernberger, P. (1996). *Strong and fearless: The quest for personal power*. St. Paul, MN: Yes International.

O'Brien, J. (1996). *A meeting of mystic paths: Christianity and yoga*. St. Paul, MN: Yes International.

Ornstein, R. (2008). *Meditation and modern psychology*. Los Altos, CA: Major Books.

Prabhavananda, S., & Isherwood, C. (1953). *How to know god*. Hollywood, CA: Vedanta Press.

Rama, S. (1992). *Meditation and its practice*. Honesdale, PA: Himalayan Institute.

Ramana Maharshi. (2000). *Talks with Ramana Maharshi: On realizing abiding peace and happiness*. Carlsbad, CA: Inner Directions.

Thera, N. (1962). *The heart of Buddhist meditation: A handbook of mental training based on the Buddha's way of mindfulness*. New York, NY: Samuel Weiser.

Tigunait, Pandit Rajmani. (1996). *The power of mantra and the mystery of initiation*. Honesdale, PA: Himalayan Publishers.

Udupa, K. (1978). *Stress and its management by yoga*. Delhi, India: Motilal Banarsidass.

Websites

Charles and Carol Crenshaw's **free** website resources for you:

Basic breath awareness and tension relaxation download: www.taptfjl.com/batr.html

Systematic relaxation instruction download: www.taptfjl.com/sr.html

Basic guided meditation download:
www.taptfjl.com/gm.html

To purchase a 4-part Introduction to Meditation Basics video
set: www.taptfjl.com/medcrse.html

Other useful websites:

www.taptfjl.com
For info on EFT sessions (Skype available)

www.MakingWeightLossEasy.com
For info on EFT and weight loss (Skype available)

www.EasilyStopSmokingNow.com
For info on smoking cessation, NLP, or hypnosis (Skype
available)

www.oils-transcend.com For info about essential oils

www.ipyc.org Inner Peace Yoga Center

Medical illustrations: Jennifer Hollis, MS,

www.hollisvisualizations.com

About the Authors

Charles B. Crenshaw Jr., MS, MDivW, is a Vietnam era veteran who has been meditating since 1974 and teaching meditation since the 1980s. His master's degree in Eastern studies, comparative psychology, and holistic health entailed in-depth study of Eastern and Western psychological paradigms and their relationship to the practice of meditation. In his studies for that degree, and subsequently, he had the opportunity to check his skills against biofeedback technologies. His primary teachers for meditation have been Dr. Swami Rama of the Himalayas, Swami Veda Bharati, Pandit Rajmani Tigunait, and other teachers of the Himalayan tradition, and he is an initiator in the tradition of Himalayan meditation masters. Charles is the author of *Pathless Path: God, Grace, Guru* (an autobiographical account of his journey with meditation and yoga) and a contributing author in the *Clinical EFT Handbook: A Definitive Resource for Practitioners, Scholars, Clinicians, and Researchers*. He also writes book reviews for the *Energy Psychology* journal. In addition, Charles is an interfaith minister (the New Seminary) specializing in spiritual counseling, a trained hypnotist and trainer, and a master neuro-linguistic programming (NLP) practitioner and trainer, and has trained as a substance abuse counselor. He is cofounder and codirector of the Inner Peace Yoga Center, an educational nonprofit organization in Indianapolis, Indiana. Charles has also been on the faculty of the College of Humanities and Sciences at the University of Phoenix where he taught courses in Eastern and Western religion. He is a certified EFT practitioner and a Touch for Health practitioner.

Carol E. Crenshaw, MS, EdM, has been meditating since 1978 and teaching meditation since the 1980s. Her graduate degree in Eastern studies, comparative psychology, and holistic health involved the in-depth study of Eastern and Western psychological paradigms and their relationship to the practice of meditation. Her primary teachers for meditation have been Swami Rama of the Himalayas, Swami Veda Bharati, Pandit Rajmani Tigunait, and other teachers of the Himalayan tradition, and she is an initiator in the tradition of Himalayan meditation masters. She is the cofounder and codirector of the Inner Peace Yoga Center in Indianapolis. Carol is a contributing author in the *Clinical EFT Handbook: A Definitive Resource for Practitioners, Scholars, Clinicians, and Researchers* and has written articles for *Yoga International, Himalayan News, Himalayan Path,* and *OM Indiana* as well as book reviews for *Energy Psychology*. Carol is a former elementary school teacher and former adjunct faculty in the College of Humanities and Sciences at the University of Phoenix. She is a consulting hypnotist and certified practitioner in Emotional Freedom Techniques (EFT), neuro-linguistic programming (NLP), and Touch for Health.

For further information, please contact us:

Charles: (317) 525-6539

Carol: (317) 445-4203

Email: trainers@taptfjl.com

Our websites:

www.taptfjl.com

www.MakingWeightLossEasy.com

www.EasilyStopSmokingNow.com

www.oils-transcend.com

2198231862172323